Supplemental
SAP Labs and Textbook
Spring 2016

For Courses Utilizing

HEC Montréal's
ERP Simulation Game
Manufacturing Game
Powered by ERPsim

Tim Rutherford, MBA

Table Of Contents

By Tim Rutherford: linkedin.com/in/timrutherford/

Cover photo: Léger, P.-M., Robert, J., Babin, G., Pellerin, R. and Wagner, B. (2007), ERPsim, ERPsim Lab, HEC Montréal, Montréal, Qc.

This supplemental text contains references to the products and intellectual property of HEC Montreal's ERPsim Lab. The names of these products are registered and/or unregistered trademarks of HEC Montreal's ERPsim Lab. HEC Montreal's ERPsim Lab is neither the author nor the publisher of this book and is not responsible for its content.

All ERPsim references, screen shots, and implications: Léger, P.-M., Robert, J., Babin, G., Pellerin, R. and Wagner, B. (2007), ERPsim, ERPsim Lab, HEC Montréal, Montréal, Qc.

This supplemental text contains references to the products of SAP AG, Dietmar-Hopp-Allee 16, 69190 Walldorf, Germany. The names of these products are registered and/or unregistered trademarks of SAP AG. SAP AG is neither the author nor the publisher of this book and is not responsible for its content.

This Textbook's Screen Shots

SAP frequently releases new versions of its SAP GUI (Graphical User Interface). This is the typical interface most people use to interact with the SAP ERP system.

While the new releases of the GUI typically include "behind the scenes" updates, the most recent update, SAPGUI 7.40, includes some visual changes.

This supplemental textbook utilizes screen shots from prior releases of the SAP GUI. This should not create an issue for students following along with the included exercises as the visualizations are different, but the functionality is the same.

Of the many visual changes within this release, the most noticeable change comes from the toolbar's new look. Functionality is entirely the same as it was, but the buttons look different.

Previous toolbar:

SAPGUI 740 toolbar:

The location of the buttons, the functionality of the buttons, and the names of the buttons have all remained constant. Please note these differences as you continue with these labs. By the time you get through a few pages, you likely won't even notice the difference.

Once the new GUI has been adopted across most of the SAP University Alliance member institutions, this supplemental textbook will be updated with new screen shots.

Part I

SAP Navigation

and

SAP Labs

Logging on to SAP

Before You Log On

In order to log on to SAP, you will need a fair amount of information. Once you've done this a few times it will be easier. Let's start by getting your specific information.

Find your name on the class list provided by your instructor:

	Roster Name	Signature		Group	Co.	SimID	Lab Material	Lab Product
Group 1	John Lennon	Your Group Number	→	1	A	A1	AA-F01	Nut
	George Harriso	Your Company Letter ($)	→		A	A2	AA-F02	Blueberry
	Paul McCartne	Your ERPsim ID ($#)	→			A3	AA-F03	Strawberry
	Richard Starke	Your Product ($$-F0#)	→				AA-F04	Raisin

From the above example, "A" will always be your company letter and, throughout ERPsim and the following labs, will be designated as "$". If you see one "$", that means your company letter or, following through with this example, "A". If you see "$$", that means "AA" (or your company letter twice). The number from your login ID will be designated as "#" throughout the following documentation. You will eventually see something like: "$$-F0#". Using the example "A1", this would translate to "AA-F01"—repeating the company letter twice and then adding your login ID's number.

Logging on to SAP

Open the SAP GUI (Graphical User Interface). It may be on your desktop, within a folder called "Applications", or within "Programs" on the Windows Start Menu. Ask your instructor if you are unable to locate this icon.

Wherever you find it, it will look like this:

Double-click on this icon. If you are using the SAP GUI within your school's computer lab, the logon screen will likely give a list of available servers/connections on the right panel.

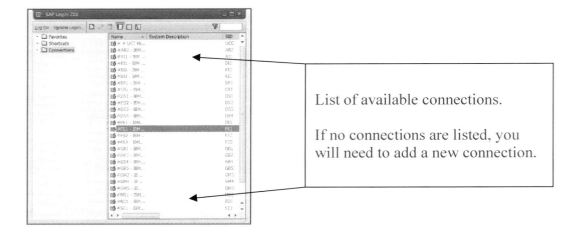

List of available connections.

If no connections are listed, you will need to add a new connection.

-If you need to add a connection-

Click on the "New" button and add the server information below.

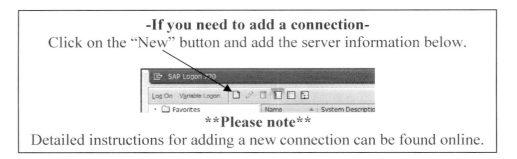

Please note

Detailed instructions for adding a new connection can be found online.

The server you choose will depend on what you are doing within SAP. Contact your instructor for your server information. Typically, your instructor will provide you with this information at the start of each class requiring SAP.

Connect to Your Server

Within the SAP logon GUI, look at the list of available connections. Find the server for the client you intend to use (provided by your instructor). Double-click on the server you will be using.

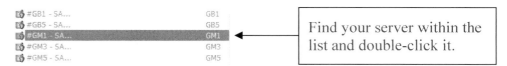

Find your server within the list and double-click it.

You will see a screen similar to this:

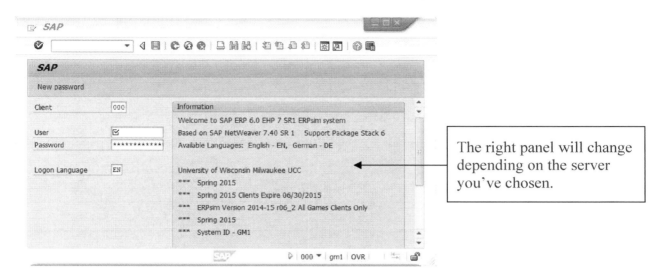

The right panel will change depending on the server you've chosen.

Add the appropriate information—provided by your instructor:

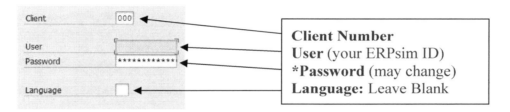

Client Number
User (your ERPsim ID)
***Password** (may change)
Language: Leave Blank

*This is a temporary password. Once you've logged on, you will be asked for a new password:

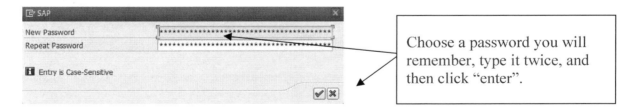

Choose a password you will remember, type it twice, and then click "enter".

Remember that we're using the "full" SAP software, which presumes that you are a regular user of the system. But, you are not. You'll be using a new SAP system nearly every week, typing a temporary password and creating a new password. Aside from the "SAP Labs", it is unlikely that you'll repeatedly log back in to the same server/client.

*Throughout the term the ERPsim client will be "refreshed" with all data deleted and reset. Each time it is refreshed, you will have to log on as if you've never logged on before and provide a new password. It's in your best interest to use the same password each time. And… no need to

make it complicated. No one will be "hacking" your SAP system. Keep it simple and memorable.

Once you've typed in a new password, several screens may pop up. Provided there are no error messages, just click enter until you reach a screen similar to this:

Congratulations! You've logged on to SAP!

Navigating SAP

The SAP GUI

All concepts, strategies, or processes you learn within this class are meant to be actualized and practiced within a "live" SAP system. SAP's GUI is functional and presumes that you know what you're doing. And why not? The typical SAP user only utilizes a handful of transactions/screens throughout their work day. To increase speed, SAP presumes that the user knows what they are doing. And that's true for the typical SAP user. Once you know the interface, you'll zip around from transaction to transaction.

But, if you've never used it before, it can be intimidating.

This course presumes that you have not used the SAP GUI before. And, even if you have used it before, this section may teach you some navigation tips you don't know.

Let's dig in!

The ERPsim Job Aid

Within this course you'll primarily be utilizing one of the ERPsim games. These games simulate a market situation within a full-blown SAP system. Typical transactions used throughout the game are included on a separate "Job Aid" specific to the game you are playing. Your instructor will provide this for you when you are playing one of the games.

The Job Aid lists transaction codes and then brief instructions for completing each transaction.

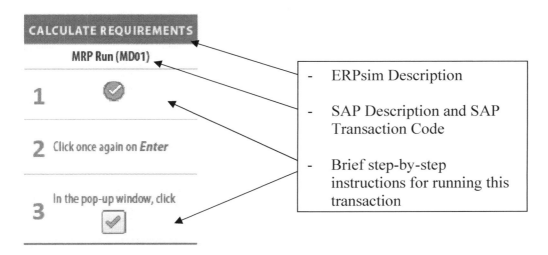

Transaction codes allow for quick maneuvering from transaction screen to transaction screen. With some practice, and more experience, you'll likely start to memorize these transaction codes.

Now that you have the code, what do you do with it?

Transaction codes are entered directly into the SAP GUI.

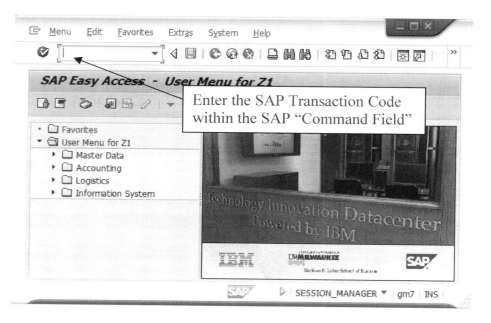

Can't find the command field? Sometimes it's hidden.

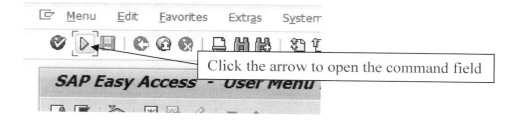

Practice: SAP Navigation

Transaction Code: CS12

You'll notice that the menu screen disappears and you're instantly in the transaction "CS12".

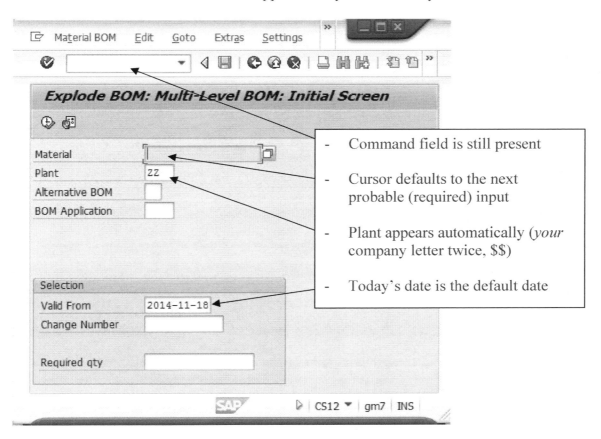

Return to the main SAP Menu by clicking the back arrow.

Let's try a different transaction.

Transaction Code: VA01

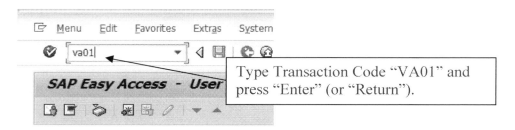

As you execute the new transaction, the SAP Menu disappears.

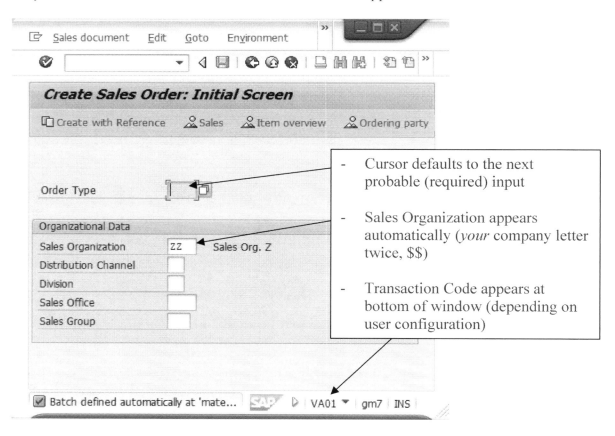

The SAP GUI allows you to interact with one transaction at a time. In order to move from one transaction to another, you have two choices:

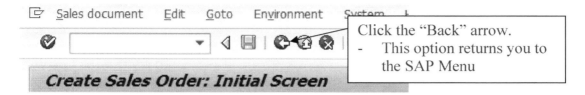

Click the "Back" arrow.
- This option returns you to the SAP Menu

or

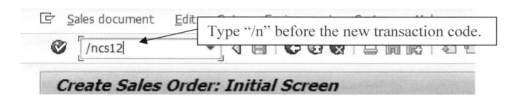

Type "/n" before the new transaction code.

Typing "/n" before the new transaction code tells the SAP GUI to close the current transaction and then move to the new transaction. This bypasses the SAP Menu.

If you haven't already, try typing "/ncs12" into the SAP Menu's Command Field.

You should find yourself in the new transaction, CS12 "Explode BOM".

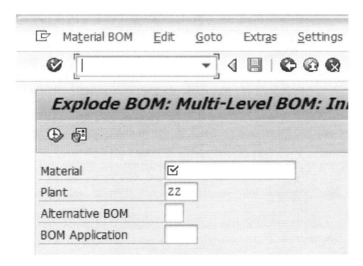

Within the Command Field, type "/nva01" to return to the "Create Sales Order" transaction.

New Sessions

Throughout the SAP Labs, and most certainly during ERPsim gameplay, you will need to have multiple windows opened at once. In order to run a new transaction – while keeping the current

transaction window open – you'll have to open a new window. SAP refers to these windows as "Sessions".

To open a new window, click the "New Session" button.

A new SAP Menu opens within a new window.

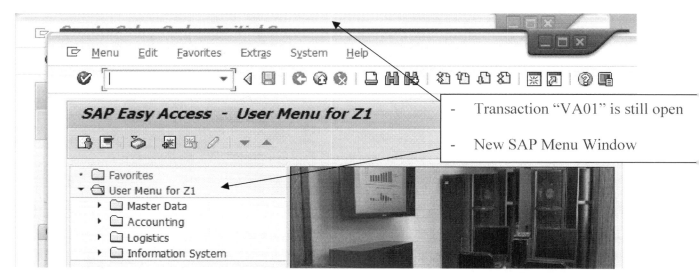

The SAP GUI allows each user to run SIX separate sessions/windows. As you play the ERPsim games, you'll learn which transactions are required for your specific activities, and which of those transactions should be opened in new sessions.

But wait, there's more...

This section is not meant to exhaustively cover SAP navigation but to give you enough of a background to get started in SAP. The following SAP Labs give you step-by-step instructions for navigating SAP. Read the directions carefully.

> Note: the following labs presume that you're learning as you go and that you require fewer and fewer "step-by-step" instructions. By Lab 03, it presumes you learned the basic navigation detailed in Lab 01. Pay attention, read, and learn as you go.

Lab 01 - Production
Forecast to Finished Goods

Within this lab you will create 1000 of your specific product, from nothing to something.

First, let's determine what your product will be. What is your company letter?

Your company letter is determined by taking the alphabetical equivalent of your official group number. As an example, Group 1 will be Company "A". Group 4 will be Company "D".

Second—what is your logon ID for ERPsim? It *should* start with your company letter followed by a number, presumably between 1-4 (A1, B3, C2, etc.). Within all of our examples, we'll be using V1.

Those two bits of information will determine which product you'll be creating and selling within these lab exercises. Presume that your ERPsim login ID is "A1".

From that, "A" will always be your company letter and, throughout ERPsim and these labs, will be designated as "$". If you see one "$", that means your company letter or, following through with this example, "A". If you see "$$", that means "AA" (or your company letter twice). The number from your login ID will be designated as "#" throughout the following documentation. You will eventually see something like: "$$-F0#". Using the example "A1", this would translate to "AA-F01"—repeating the company letter twice and then adding your login ID's number.

Whatever your company letter may be, the number will designate which finished good you will be creating and selling within the following labs.

All finished goods use the "material number" format: $$-F0# ("using "A1", "AA-F01")

Within the ERPsim Manufacturing Game, each team starts with the following six products:

$$-F01 – Nut Muesli 1.0 kg.
$$-F02 – Blueberry Muesli 1.0 kg.
$$-F03 – Strawberry Muesli 1.0 kg.
$$-F04 – Raisin Muesli 1.0 kg.
$$-F05 – Original Muesli 1.0 kg.
$$-F06 – Mixed Fruit Muesli 1.0 kg.

Which product will you be working with within these exercises? The product whose number matches your login ID. If your login ID is $1, you'll be working with "$$-F01", if it's $2, "$$-F02", etc. Remember, when you see "$" you will always replace this with your company letter.

If you still need some help determining your company or your product, ask a group member* or refer back to the class list (provided by your instructor):

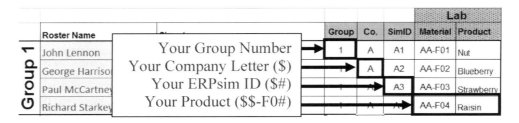

	Roster Name		Group	Co.	SimID	Material	Product
Group 1	John Lennon	Your Group Number	1	A	A1	AA-F01	Nut
	George Harrison	Your Company Letter ($)		A	A2	AA-F02	Blueberry
	Paul McCartney	Your ERPsim ID ($#)			A3	AA-F03	Strawberry
	Richard Starkey	Your Product ($$-F0#)				AA-F04	Raisin

Do you have your product? Great—now let's go produce it!

*Note: These labs are set up presuming that you are working within a group. If you are not, just ignore the references to your "group".

The BOM – Bill of Material

The BOM (Bill of Material) is the "ingredients list", or, the overall "recipe" for this product. Let's look at the ingredients within your product. Within all of our examples / screen shots, we will be producing "VV-F06", or Mixed Fruit Muesli 1.0 kg. for Company V. Be sure to change this to YOUR company and your personal product.

Type the following SAP Transaction Code into the SAP Command Field (refer to the previous section, "SAP Navigation", if you do not know how to do this):

Transaction Code: CS12

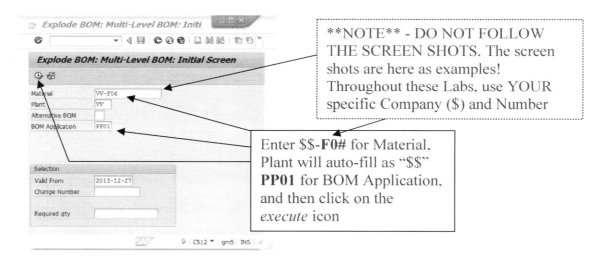

NOTE - DO NOT FOLLOW THE SCREEN SHOTS. The screen shots are here as examples! Throughout these Labs, use YOUR specific Company ($) and Number

Enter $$-**F0#** for Material, Plant will auto-fill as "$$" **PP01** for BOM Application, and then click on the *execute* icon

This will display the BOM for *your* product:

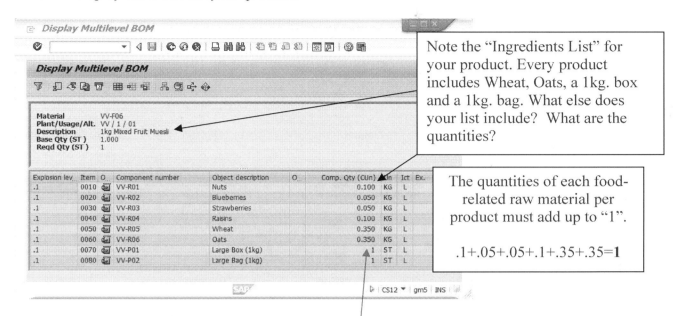

Note the "Ingredients List" for your product. Every product includes Wheat, Oats, a 1kg. box and a 1kg. bag. What else does your list include? What are the quantities?

The quantities of each food-related raw material per product must add up to "1".

.1+.05+.05+.1+.35+.35=**1**

Remember, this is the "ingredients list" for producing **one** box of your muesli product.

For your product ($$-F0#), we want to manufacture 1000 finished products. You will need to order enough of each ingredient/material to manufacture 1000 finished products. How many of each listed material should you order? It's easy to calculate this. From your BOM, how many of the following ingredients are required to create 1000 finished products?

Based on the BOM, complete the following ingredients list for 1000 of your product:

Ingredient	Component Number	Qty / Product	x 1000	Total to Order
wheat			x 1000	
oat			x 1000	
raisin			x 1000	
nut			x 1000	
strawberry			x 1000	
blueberry			x 1000	
box			x 1000	
bag			x 1000	

The above chart is the "grocery list" for your product. You want to create 1000 of your product and this is what you have to buy in order to complete the product. *Note that this is a portion of MRP—Material Requirements Planning. You'll see more of this as we start the ERPsim games.

Calculate the raw material requirements for your product and let's go shopping!

Open a new session (leaving the BOM) screen open.

Create Purchase Order

Transaction Code: ME21N

Which will bring up the following screen:

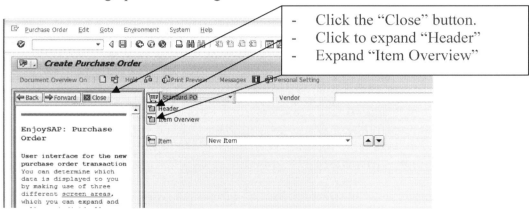

- Click the "Close" button.
- Click to expand "Header"
- Expand "Item Overview"

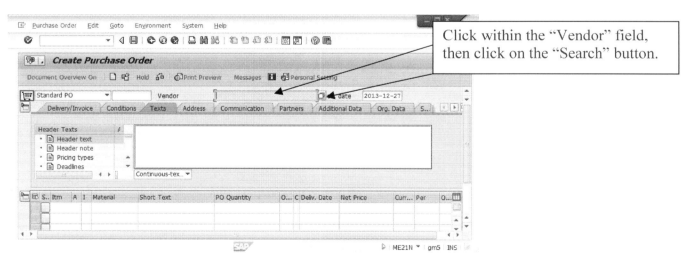

Click within the "Vendor" field, then click on the "Search" button.

Clicking the "search" button brings up the following screen:

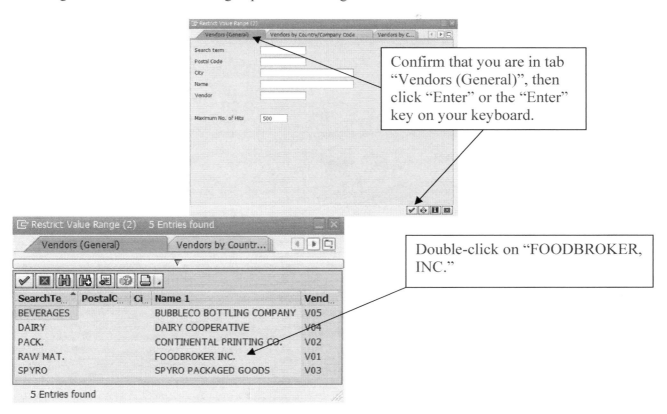

Confirm that you are in tab "Vendors (General)", then click "Enter" or the "Enter" key on your keyboard.

Double-click on "FOODBROKER, INC."

We will need to create two purchase orders (POs), one for the food materials and the other for the packaging requirements – the boxes and bags.

Double-click on "FOODBROKER, INC.", which will bring you back to the PO page.

Note that "FOODBROKER, INC." has been replaced by a "Vendor Number".

Click "enter" to validate the PO.

The vendor name "FOODBROKER, INC." has been replaced by a vendor number. SAP utilizes

a master record for information that does not change that often, such as customer and vendor names and numbers. This vendor's information has been consolidated down to a simple three character code.

After clicking "Enter", the error: "Enter Purch. Group" will display. Type "100" for "Raw Materials" and press enter.

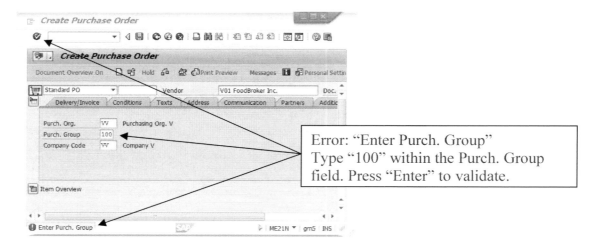

Error: "Enter Purch. Group"
Type "100" within the Purch. Group field. Press "Enter" to validate.

From here, type your grocery list—but only for **FOOD ITEMS**. We'll need to create a separate PO for the boxes and bags. Be very careful to type the amounts and the "Material" EXACTLY as it is listed within the BOM. Remember that you have the BOM open in another window if you need to double-check a material code or quantity.

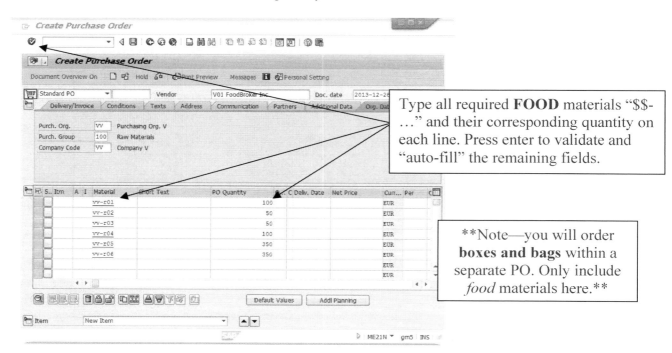

Type all required **FOOD** materials "$$-…" and their corresponding quantity on each line. Press enter to validate and "auto-fill" the remaining fields.

Note—you will order **boxes and bags** within a separate PO. Only include *food* materials here.**

Click "Enter" after adding all materials and quantities. Correct any errors—if you can. Sometimes it's easier just to re-start this process rather than correct multiple errors. Don't worry—it'll move more quickly the 2nd time you do this.

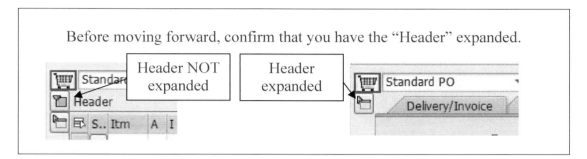

You'll see that many of the fields are "auto-populated" based on the Vendor, material code, and the quantity. This is an example of how the "common database" within SAP makes an individual's work easier. It would take a long time to type all of this information. However, with a common database, this information is auto-populated within each field automatically.

Double-check your work. Are you sure that your quantities are correct?

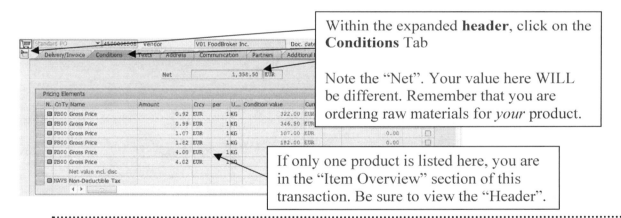

Within the expanded **header**, click on the **Conditions** Tab

Note the "Net". Your value here WILL be different. Remember that you are ordering raw materials for *your* product.

If only one product is listed here, you are in the "Item Overview" section of this transaction. Be sure to view the "Header".

> ***The following is not "busy work" nor "information only"***
> Bookmark this page and find the *Relevant Information* form at the end of this Supplemental Text. It should be the final page of the textbook. If you are unable to locate it, check the Table of Contents for its page number.
>
> This *Relevant Information* form is used to log your lab information, either for troubleshooting or for other areas of this or future labs.
>
> In the area provided on the *Relevant Information* form, write this net amount on line 1.1 and then come back to this page. The "Net" amount here will be necessary within SAP Lab 03. (Note: you're also about to write the value for line 1.2…)

Do your numbers look okay? If so, click "Save" on the toolbar (floppy disc) and the click "save" on the resulting question box:

A message on the bottom of your SAP screen will appear:

☑ Standard PO created under the number 4500000004

> On the *Relevant Information* form, located at the end of this textbook, write this PO Number on line 1.2.

Do not close out of the "Create Purchase Order" screen. Remember, we still need to order bags and boxes.

From here, click the "vendor" search button again:

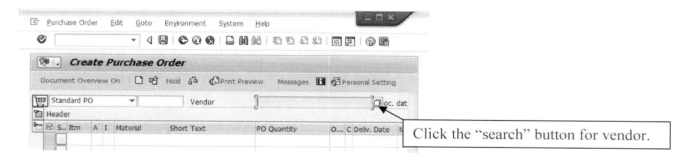

Click "Enter" on the next screen, and then double-click on "Continental Printing Co."

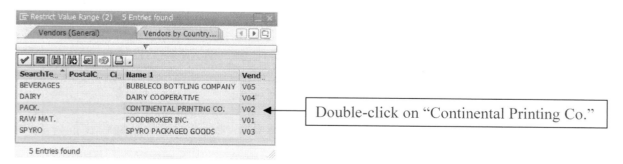

Complete the PO with 1000 boxes, and 1000 bags. Click "Enter". Remember that you will need to add "100" as the "Purch. Group".

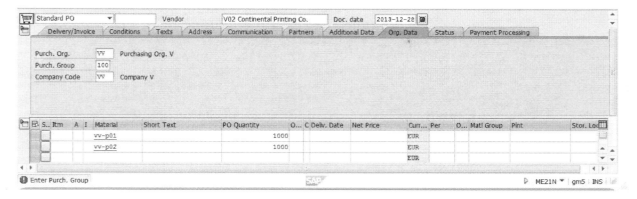

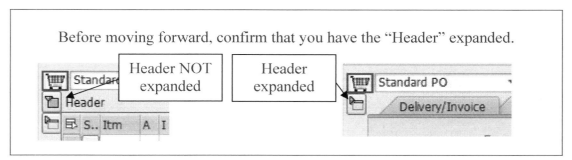

Before moving forward, confirm that you have the "Header" expanded.

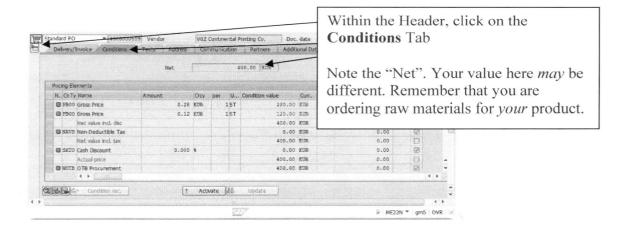

Within the Header, click on the **Conditions** Tab

Note the "Net". Your value here *may* be different. Remember that you are ordering raw materials for *your* product.

On the *Relevant Information* form, located at the end of this textbook's Part I, write this *Net Amount* on line 1.3.

Click "Enter" to have SAP auto-populate the remaining fields. If you typed everything correctly (remember that you can use the BOM screen to confirm the material codes), the PO should be ready to go. Click "Save" and then "Save" again to save the document and process the data.

On the *Relevant Information* form, located at the end of this textbook, write this *PO Number* on line 1.4.

Click the back button until you reach the "SAP Menu".

While in "real life" it could take several weeks to receive our order, and within ERPsim it takes 3-5 simulated days to receive an order, we're going to "spoof" the system and receive the order today.

From the SAP Menu,

Transaction Code: MIGO

Which will bring up the following screen:

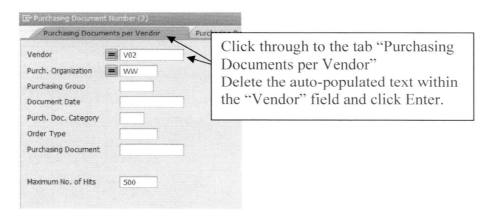

If you are searching for the PO, a search screen pops up. It may be auto-populated with a vendor:

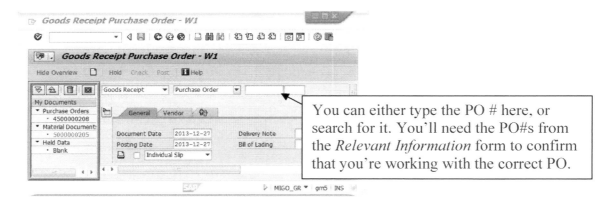

This is searching for all POs within your company (meaning your group members). You could (and probably will) find several other POs within the search results. Double-click on the PO# from "FOODBROKERAGE, INC" which you wrote down on the *Relevant Information* form.

Only complete one vendor's PO at a time. DO NOT try to work with all POs at once!

Take the time to read this sentence.

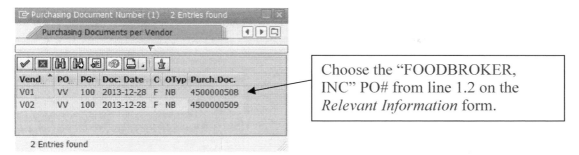

Choose the "FOODBROKER, INC" PO# from line 1.2 on the *Relevant Information* form.

Click "Enter" to auto-populate the Goods Receipt screen with all of the items on the PO.

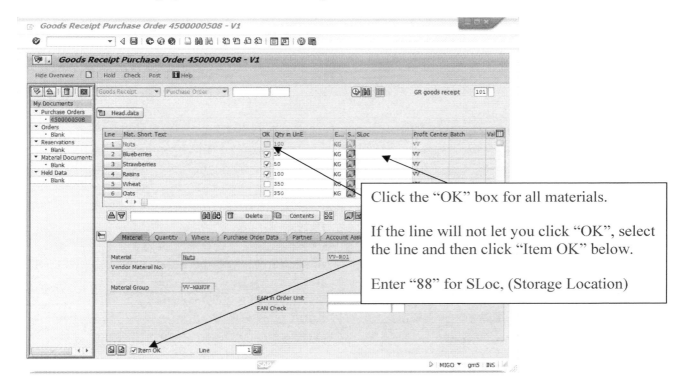

Click the "OK" box for all materials.

If the line will not let you click "OK", select the line and then click "Item OK" below.

Enter "88" for SLoc, (Storage Location)

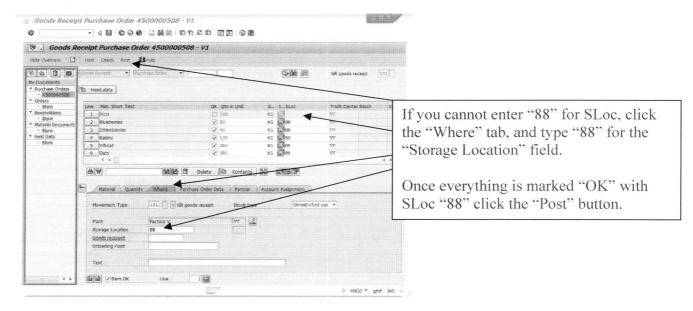

If you cannot enter "88" for SLoc, click the "Where" tab, and type "88" for the "Storage Location" field.

Once everything is marked "OK" with SLoc "88" click the "Post" button.

Repeat this process for the 2ⁿᵈ PO# (line 1.4) with CONTINENTAL PRINTING:

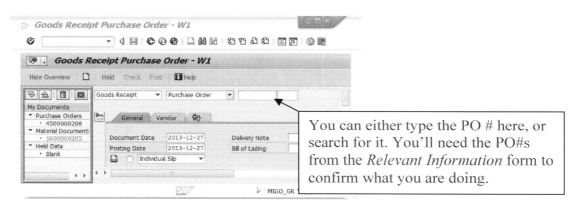

You can either type the PO # here, or search for it. You'll need the PO#s from the *Relevant Information* form to confirm what you are doing.

If you are searching for the PO, a search screen pops up. It may be auto-populated with a vendor:

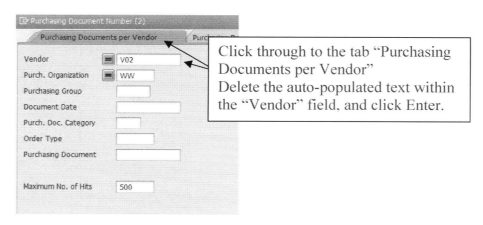

Click through to the tab "Purchasing Documents per Vendor"
Delete the auto-populated text within the "Vendor" field, and click Enter.

This is searching for all POs within your company (meaning your group members). You could (and probably will) find several other POs within the search results. Double-click on the PO# from "Continental Printing" which you wrote down on the *Relevant Information* form.

Only complete one PO at a time. DO NOT try to work with all POs at once!

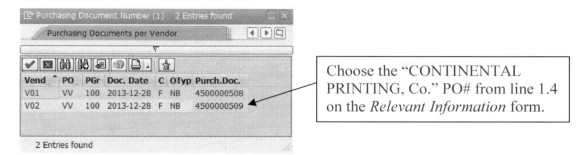

Click "Enter" to auto-populate the Goods Receipt screen with all of the items on the PO.

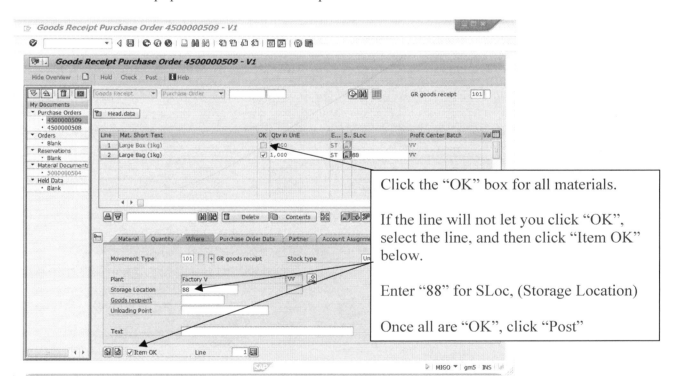

After clicking "post", click the "Back" button until you reach the main SAP Menu. Confirm that your product's raw materials are now in stock by viewing the Stock/Requirements List:

Transaction Code: MD04

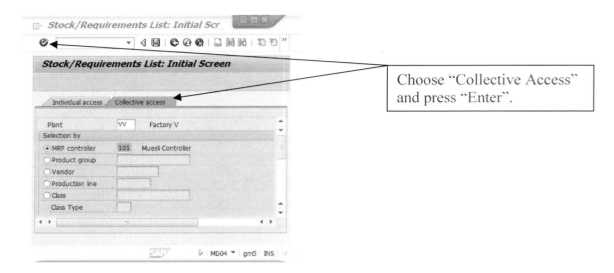

Choose "Collective Access" and press "Enter".

Notice the stock of finished goods and raw materials. Recall that the rest of your group is also working on this lab. You may see your exact number of raw materials, and you may see a wide variety of raw materials. Exact completion of this lab is very important as you'll be using raw materials in stock. If you ordered too few of a raw material and your group members order the correct amount, you *could* be using their raw materials to finish your product.

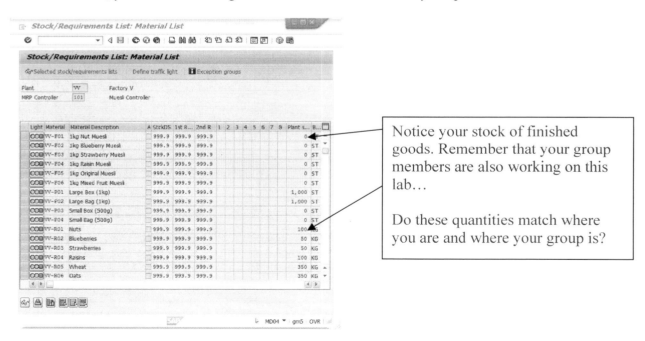

Notice your stock of finished goods. Remember that your group members are also working on this lab…

Do these quantities match where you are and where your group is?

Confirm with your group members that these numbers are accurate. If not, you may inadvertently throw off your group member's labs!

If everything looks correct, and your group members agree, click on your product and then click the "Selected stock/requirements lists".

Before we move forward, take a look at the Stock/Requirements List. It's important that you understand what you are seeing here.

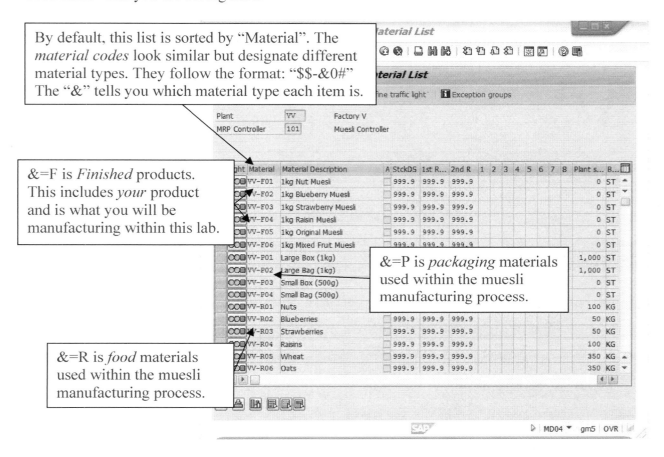

Within the Stock/Requirements list, find *your* product. Do note that your product's "Material Description" includes "1kg XXXX Muesli". The Material Code includes an "F" for "Finished Product". The Material Code looks like this: "$$-**F**0#".

Within the next step of this lab, if you were to pick the *food* raw material associated with *your* finished product, you're setting up SAP to manufacture that raw material. As an example, if you pick "Raisins", "$$-**R**04", you're telling SAP that within your manufacturing plant, you'd like to manufacture raisins. Obviously no one "manufactures" raisins. Within this lab, we order raisins from Foodbroker, Inc. Instead, you must pick *your* product, "1kg Raisin Muesli", "$$-**F**04".

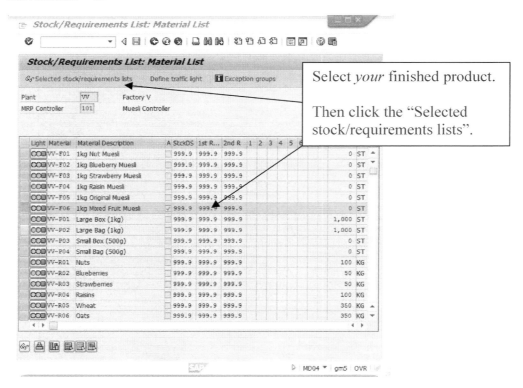

Select *your* finished product.

Then click the "Selected stock/requirements lists".

The Stock/Requirements List is specific to your product and shows your available quantity.

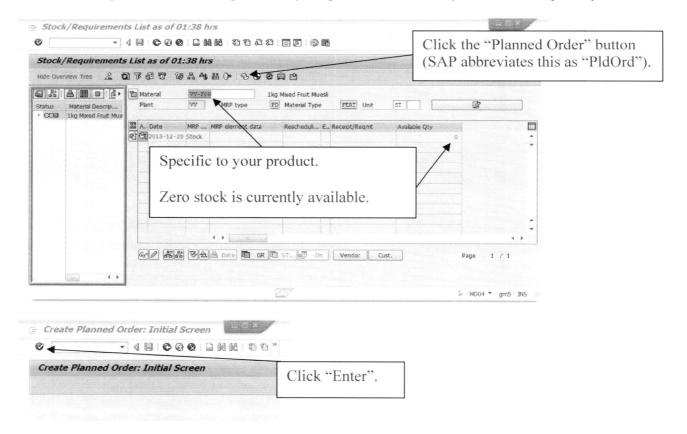

Click the "Planned Order" button (SAP abbreviates this as "PldOrd").

Specific to your product.

Zero stock is currently available.

Click "Enter".

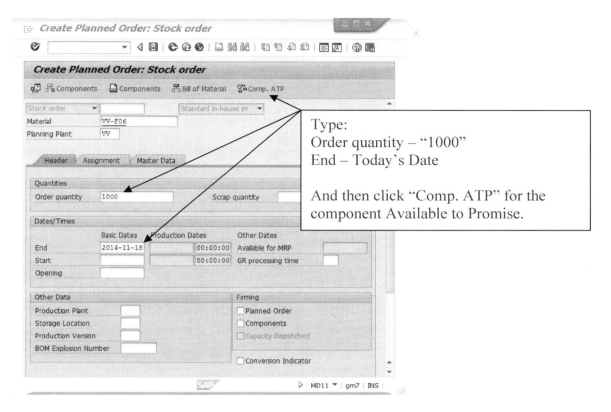

This ATP check looks at the BOM and your Order Quantity and then confirms that you have enough raw materials to complete this Production Order.

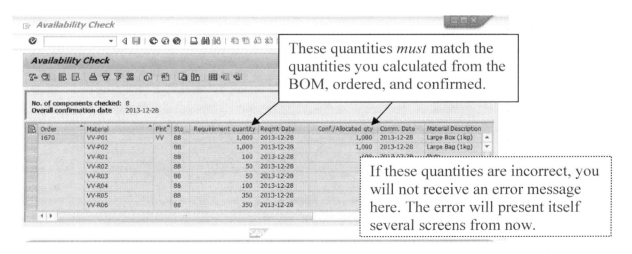

If there are any errors, retrace your steps. Did you miss something somewhere? Don't be afraid to start over. The worst thing that can happen if you start over is that you have too many raw materials. Too many raw materials is not a problem. Too few <u>is</u> a problem. Try to figure out what is wrong, fix it, and don't hesitate to re-start this lab. Sometimes restarting is easier than trying to fix issues.

If there are no errors and everything looks okay, click the back arrow to return to the "Create Planned Order: Stock order" screen. If everything is okay, click the "Save" button.

SAP will give a small confirmation on the bottom of the screen:

☑ Planned order 1670 will be created

Write this *Planned Order #* on line 1.5 of the *Relevant Information* form.

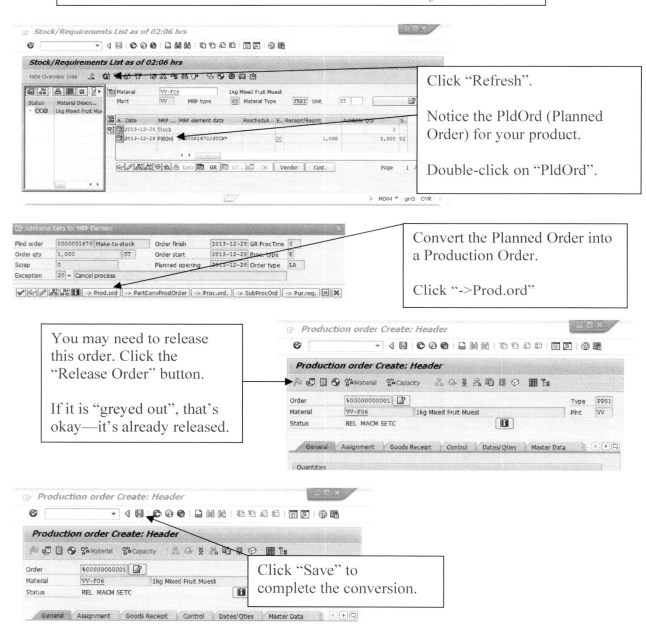

Click "Refresh".

Notice the PldOrd (Planned Order) for your product.

Double-click on "PldOrd".

Convert the Planned Order into a Production Order.

Click "->Prod.ord"

You may need to release this order. Click the "Release Order" button.

If it is "greyed out", that's okay—it's already released.

Click "Save" to complete the conversion.

You'll receive a message similar to this:

Write this *Prod. Order #* on line 1.6 of the *Relevant Information* form.

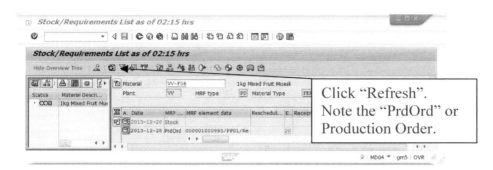

Click "Refresh".
Note the "PrdOrd" or Production Order.

Within the "real world", you would never create a production order and then immediately confirm it. Depending on the product, this could take several hours, several days, several weeks, several months... you get the idea. But, through the magic of academics, we'll pretend that this production order will be completed within mere moments.

Open a new session by clicking the "Creates New Session" button:

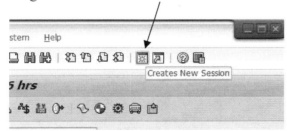

Confirm this production order:

Transaction Code: Co15

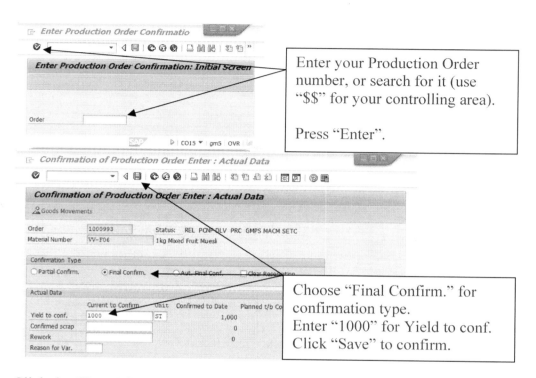

Enter your Production Order number, or search for it (use "$$" for your controlling area).

Press "Enter".

Choose "Final Confirm." for confirmation type.
Enter "1000" for Yield to conf.
Click "Save" to confirm.

Click the "Enter" button on the "Enter Production Order Confirmation" screen. You should receive a message similar to this:

☑ Confirmation saved (Goods movements: 6, failed: 0)

If it says "Confirmation saved", but also includes failed movements, fear not. Your product should be available. If you do not receive some form of the above message, re-trace your steps. Did you miss something along the way?

Switch to your other SAP window with the "Stock/Requirements List".

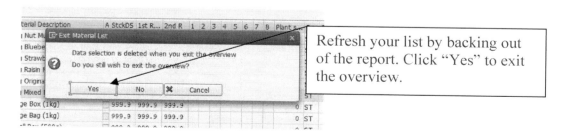

Refresh your list by backing out of the report. Click "Yes" to exit the overview.

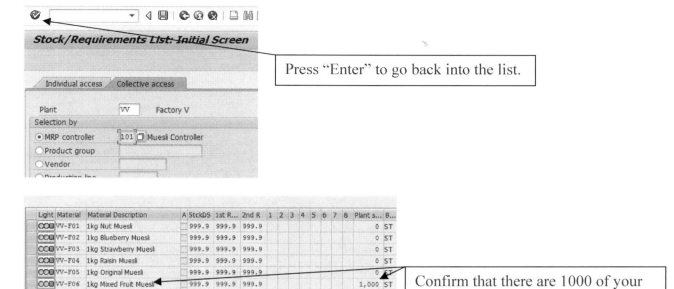

You should now have 1000 of your product produced and available for sale.

Use your (print screen) key on your keyboard to copy the Stock/requirements list: Material list. Open MS Word and paste the screen shot into the word file.

Submit this Word file into your LMT (D2L, Blackboard, Canvas, etc.) under the "Lab 01" assignment.

Save the file as:

"Last_Name - $# - Lab 01" (i.e., "Rutherford – V6 - Lab 01")

Make a note of where you are saving your file.

If you are using a computer lab: if you log off or are logged off for inactivity before uploading this file, you may lose the file.

Upload this file to your LMT under the LABS / LAB 01 assignment.

No printed copies will be accepted.

Lab 02 - Sales Order to Delivery

Now that you've created 1000 of your product, let's make a sale!

You <u>MUST</u> successfully <u>complete</u> <u>SAP Lab 01</u> before starting this lab.

Following the same instructions as Lab 01, you will be continuing with your Company Letter and Login ID Number (A1, B3, C2, etc.). Within all of our examples, we'll be using V6.

Those two bits of information should carry through from your Production lab, Lab 01. If you're using a different login ID, THIS LAB WILL NOT WORK unless you've produced 1000 products that correspond with your User ID.

To determine which product you'll be selling within these lab exercises, presume that your ERPsim login ID is "A1".

All finished goods use the "material number" format: $$-F0# ("using "A1", "AA-F01")

Do you have your product? Is this the product you manufactured within the previous lab?

Great—now let's go sell it!

Creating a SalesOrder

Transaction Code: VA01

You'll be presented with the Create Sales Order: Initial Screen:

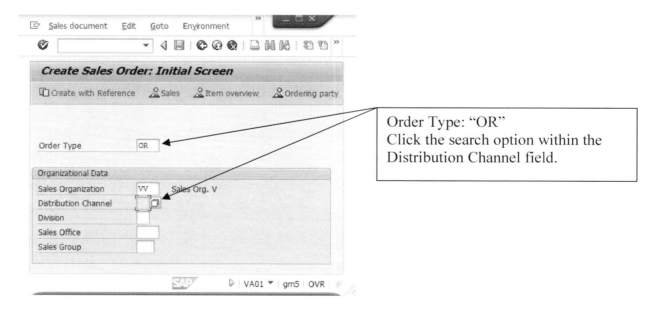

Order Type: "OR"
Click the search option within the Distribution Channel field.

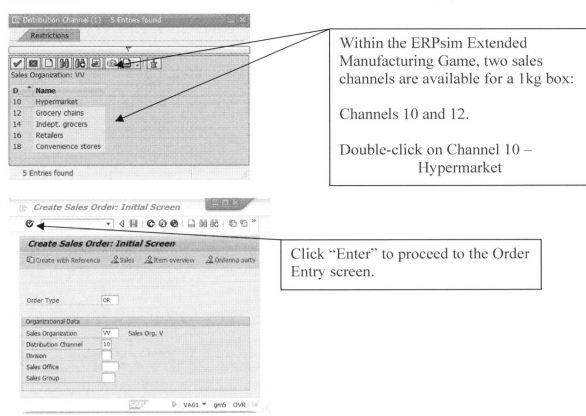

Within the ERPsim Extended Manufacturing Game, two sales channels are available for a 1kg box:

Channels 10 and 12.

Double-click on Channel 10 – Hypermarket

Click "Enter" to proceed to the Order Entry screen.

The following screen offers all information required to create a sales order. As you'll see, the *common database* used within SAP comes in quite handy for the salesperson taking this order.

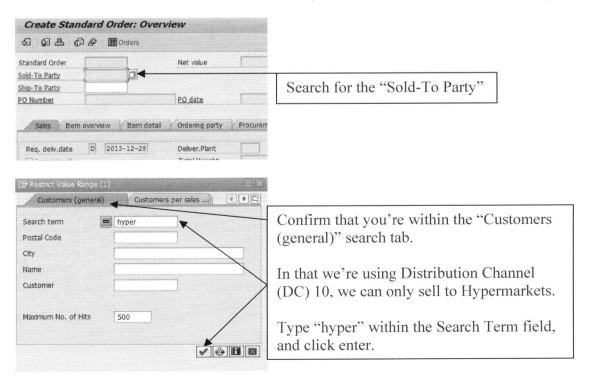

Search for the "Sold-To Party"

Confirm that you're within the "Customers (general)" search tab.

In that we're using Distribution Channel (DC) 10, we can only sell to Hypermarkets.

Type "hyper" within the Search Term field, and click enter.

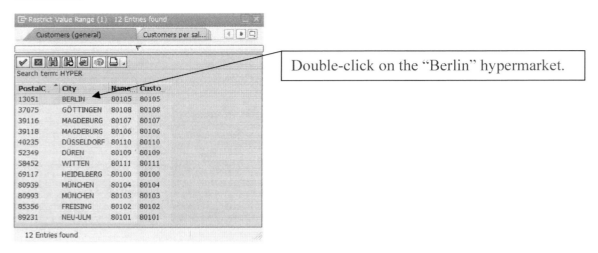

Double-click on the "Berlin" hypermarket.

Click on the "Enter" button to validate and auto-fill information for this Sold-To Party.

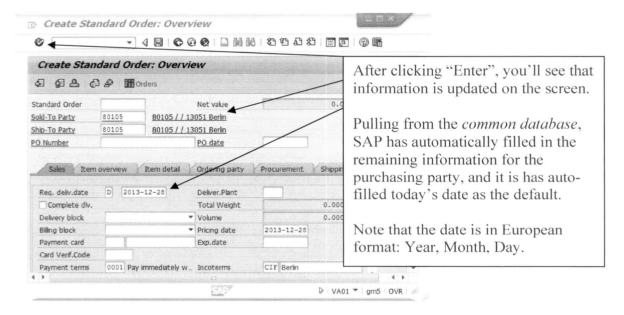

After clicking "Enter", you'll see that information is updated on the screen.

Pulling from the *common database*, SAP has automatically filled in the remaining information for the purchasing party, and it is has auto-filled today's date as the default.

Note that the date is in European format: Year, Month, Day.

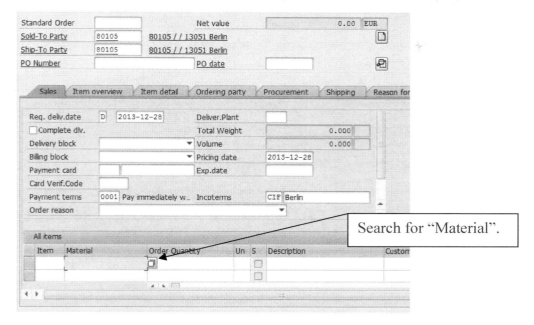

Search for "Material".

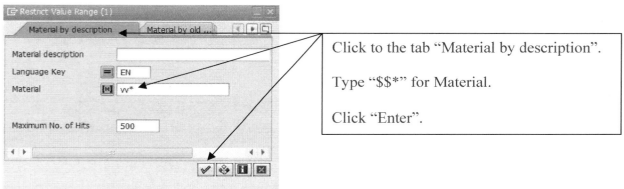

Click to the tab "Material by description".

Type "$$*" for Material.

Click "Enter".

The results may be surprising to you. There is a long list of materials that will pop up here. This not only includes the Finished Products and Raw Materials for the Manufacturing Game, but also the various products available within all of the ERPsim games, including the Distribution Game and the Logistics game.

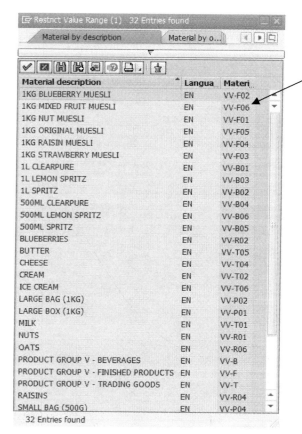

Double-click on the product that corresponds with your ERPsim ID, and is the product you manufactured within SAP Lab 01.

"$$-F0#"

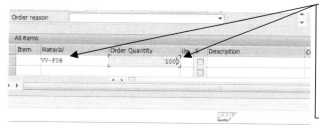

Your product, "$$-F0#", has been entered.

Type "1000" for the order quantity. (Yes, you're selling everything).

Click "Enter"

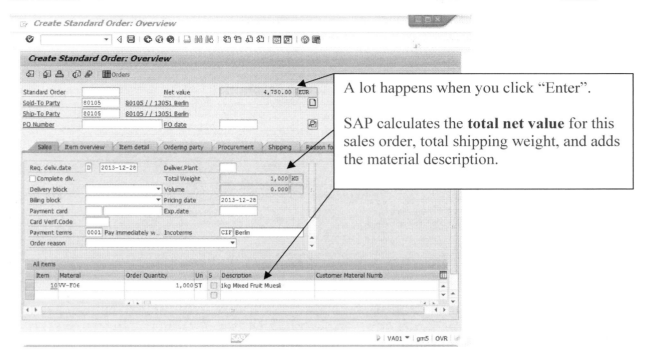

A lot happens when you click "Enter".

SAP calculates the **total net value** for this sales order, total shipping weight, and adds the material description.

> Write this order's *Net Value* on line 2.1 of the *Relevant Information* form,

But, SAP has not validated that this product is even available. At this point, if you hadn't completed SAP Lab 01, you could get this far without an error. In fact, you could place this order without an error. SAP allows companies to place orders for products that aren't available as some manufacturers create the product after the order has been placed. These are "Made to Order" manufacturers. Within ERPsim, however, we are a "Make to Stock" manufacturer, which means that we create the stock and then sell it. There are no back-orders within ERPSim. If there is no stock, the order cannot be placed.

Let's see if we have enough inventory to cover this order—before we place the order.

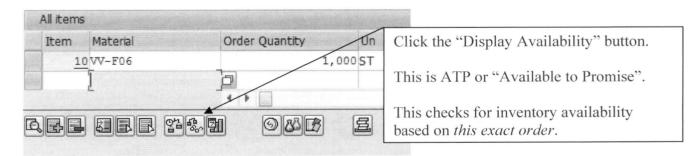

Click the "Display Availability" button.

This is ATP or "Available to Promise".

This checks for inventory availability based on *this exact order*.

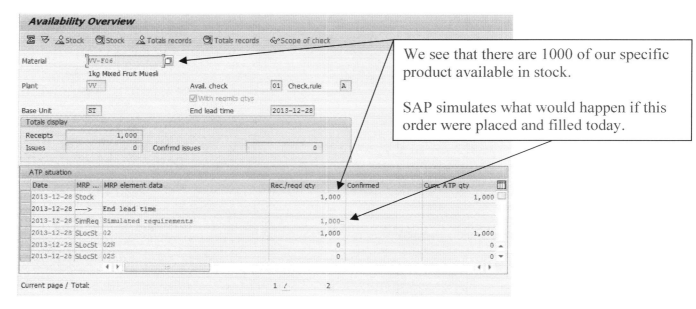

We see that there are 1000 of our specific product available in stock.

SAP simulates what would happen if this order were placed and filled today.

Within this screen, SAP simulates what would happen if the order were to be placed today, given that fulfillment states that it will ship *today*. This is important if there are multiple orders for the same product being placed at once. We don't just want to know how much is in stock, we want to know how much of that stock we can use for *our* order.

Provided you successfully completed SAP Lab 01, and you've typed everything correctly, you should see a similar screen confirming availability of your product. If you do, re-trace your steps. What did you miss? Sometimes it's easier to re-start than to try and fix a mistake. Don't be afraid to start from scratch. If you never completed SAP Lab 01, complete it before starting this lab.

If you received no errors, click "back" to the order screen, click the "Save" icon to save this order.

You will receive a message like this:

✔ Standard Order 2785 has been saved

Write this *Standard Order* # on line 2.2 of the *Relevant Information* form.

Your order has been submitted to the system, and has interacted with SAP in many areas.

Remember that the benefit of an ERP system is the *common database;* all information is available to everyone who needs it. Let's look at one area that has responded to this change.

Go back to the SAP Menu.

Transaction Code: MD04

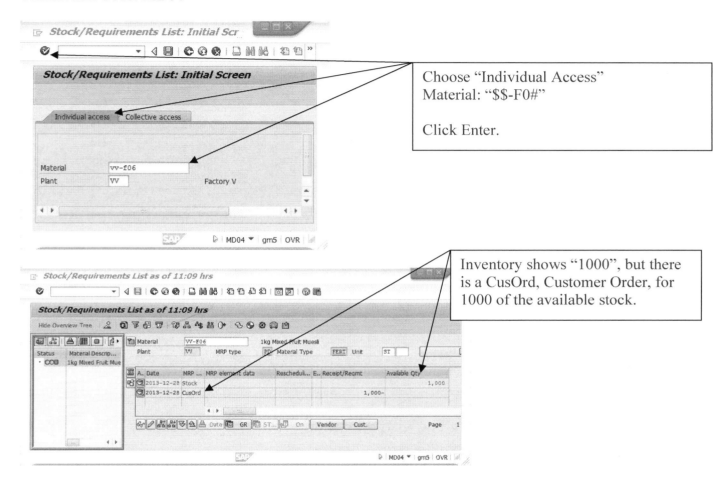

Choose "Individual Access"
Material: "$$-F0#"

Click Enter.

Inventory shows "1000", but there is a CusOrd, Customer Order, for 1000 of the available stock.

ERP systems like SAP can be configured to watch for these customer orders and alert the production manager to unexpected increases in product demand. It's important for inventory managers to do more than watch what is in stock. As we can see, there are 1000 products available, 1000 sitting "in stock", but all of them are being sold. A proactive production/inventory manager will work to replace this stock immediately.

This leads us to another issue—we have an order for *our* customer, but someone else could over-ride our order and allocate this stock to another customer. Let's allocate this to *our* customer before someone else orders it.

**Remember—it is unlikely that one person would be doing all of this. Typically, another department would take over the next few steps.

For our academic purposes, you'll wear many hats.

Create Outbound Delivery

Leave the "Stock/Requirements" window open, but create a new session.

Transaction Code: VL01N

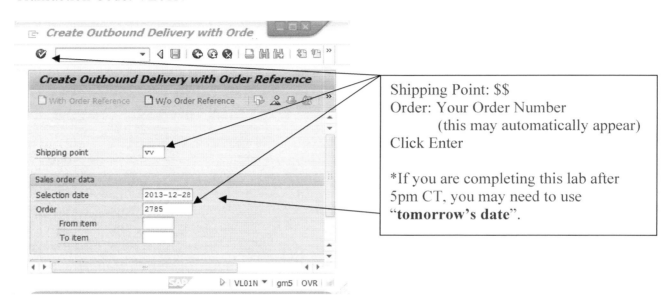

Shipping Point: $$
Order: Your Order Number
         (this may automatically appear)
Click Enter

*If you are completing this lab after 5pm CT, you may need to use **"tomorrow's date"**.

There is nothing to do on this screen except clicking "Save".

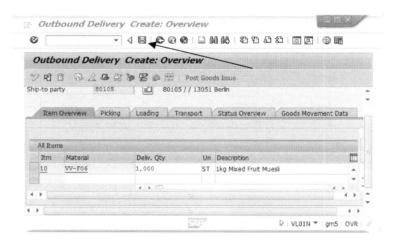

If you've been paying attention to detail, and you've seen no previous errors, you'll see a message like this:

☑ Outbound Delivery 80002784 has been saved

Write this *Outbound Delivery #* on line 2.3 of the *Relevant Information* form.

Switch back to the "Stock/Requirements List".

Click the "Refresh" button to see what this "Outbound Delivery" has done with inventory.

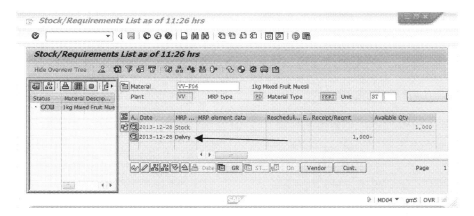

You're getting closer to claiming this inventory. It's now scheduled as a "Delivery". But, notice the stock—it's still at 1000. Someone else could still claim this inventory. The next step goes to the warehouse where someone needs to "Pick, pack, and ship" the 1000 boxes of Muesli.

Leave the "Stock/Requirements List" open and switch back to the other session.

Click "Back" until you've reached the SAP Menu.

Create Outbound Delivery – Picking your order

Transaction Code: VL02N

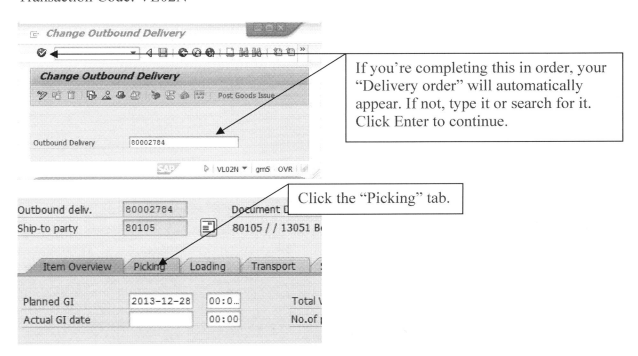

If you're completing this in order, your "Delivery order" will automatically appear. If not, type it or search for it. Click Enter to continue.

Click the "Picking" tab.

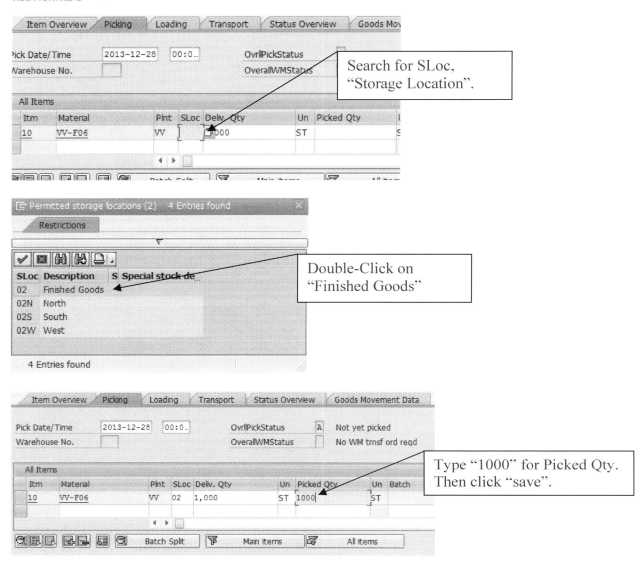

You'll receive the message:

☑ **Outbound Delivery 80002784 has been saved**

(This is the same "Outbound Delivery" you've been working with—no need to document it)

Switch to the "Stock/Requirements List" session and click the Refresh button.

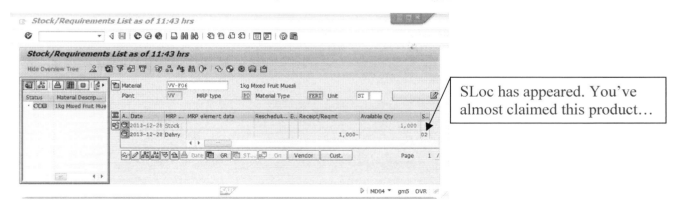

SLoc has appeared. You've almost claimed this product…

Leave the Stock/Requirements List open and switch back to your other session.

Click back until you get to the SAP Menu.

Post Goods Issue

Transaction Code: VL02N

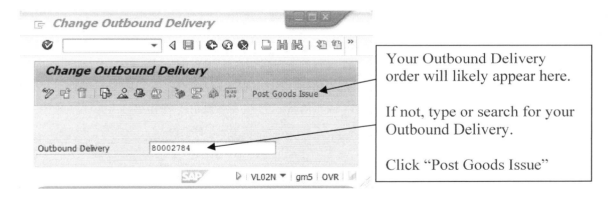

Your Outbound Delivery order will likely appear here.

If not, type or search for your Outbound Delivery.

Click "Post Goods Issue"

And, now it's officially your customer's product! Let's confirm.

Switch to the "Stock/Requirements List" and click Refresh. What do you see?

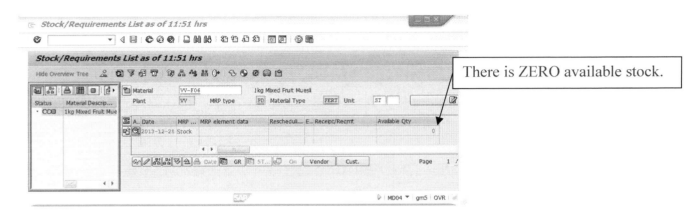

There is ZERO available stock.

The order is complete!

Switch back to the other screen—you should still be at the "Change Outbound Delivery" screen. If not:

Transaction Code: VL02N

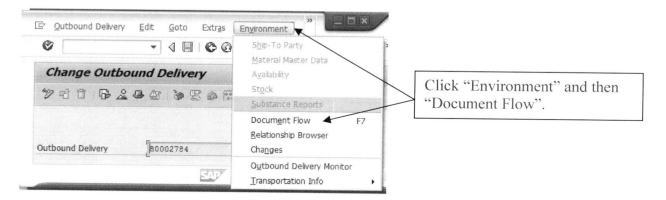

Click "Environment" and then "Document Flow".

The Document Flow is a powerful tool within SAP.

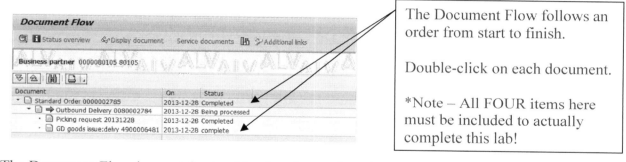

The Document Flow follows an order from start to finish.

Double-click on each document.

*Note – All FOUR items here must be included to actually complete this lab!

The Document Flow is great for trouble-shooting and tracing issues that may take place within the order entry and fulfillment process. A salesperson can check the order's status, someone in shipping can look back to see the original order. SAP gives each individual just enough information to do their portion of the process, but allows them full access to the details—as needed.

Use your (print screen) key on your keyboard to copy the completed Document Flow for your sales order. Open MS Word and paste the screen shot into the word file.

Submit this Word file into your LMT (D2L, Blackboard, Canvas, etc.) under the "Lab 02" assignment.

Save the file as:

"Last_Name - $# - Lab 02" (i.e., "Rutherford – V6 - Lab 02")

Make a note of where you are saving your file.

If you are using computer lab: if you log off or are logged off for inactivity before uploading this file, you may lose the file.

Upload this file to your LMT under the LABS / LAB 02 assignment.

No printed copies will be accepted.

Lab 03 – Accounting and Bookkeeping

No matter what you produce, or what you sell, you still have to account for the cash-flow within your company. Within this section we'll step through general accounting and cash-flow related bookkeeping, while watching ad-hoc financial statements.

> **Note – throughout this lab YOUR numbers will differ from ALL screen shots. Within SAP Lab 01, you created your own product and ordered the relevant raw materials for that product. In SAP Lab 02, you sold your product at your product's selling price. Meanwhile, your group members may have been working on the same labs with –their– products at their own prices. Here in SAP Lab 03, you'll see the financials for your company—with your information *and* your group's information. If you've documented your previous labs, as requested, you should be able to plug those numbers in and reach the same end result— complete accounting for *your* product, and hopefully accurate financial statements.**

Let's take a look at the company's financials first.

Ad-hoc Financial Statements

Transaction Code: F.01

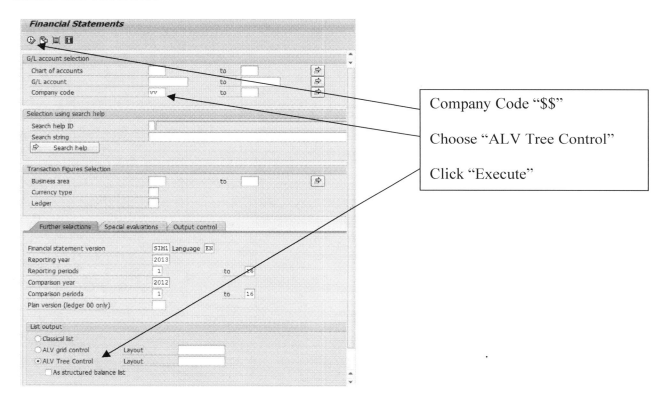

Company Code "$$"

Choose "ALV Tree Control"

Click "Execute"

You'll receive a warning, but don't pay attention to it. Click "Enter" to continue.

Remember that these statements reflect what you've been doing within SAP using this ERPsim ID; your numbers will vary. However, you should see one major item: Negative Net Income.

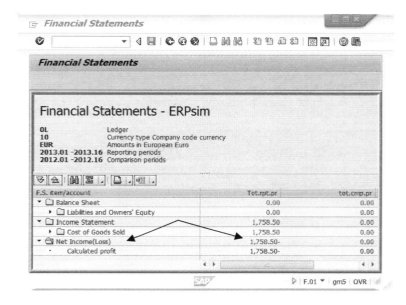

Why do you have negative net income? You've sold something, presumably at a profit. But even that sale isn't showing. Why?

Expand the following tree: **Income Statement ▷Cost of Goods Sold ▷Ending Inventory**

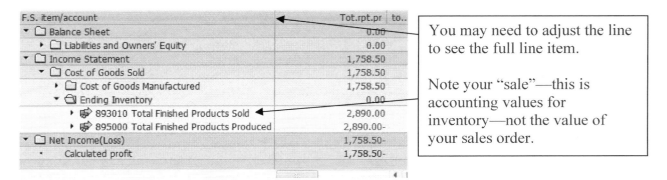

And why do you have negative net income?

Think back to what we accomplished within SAP Lab 02. We sold 1000 products, we pick-pack-and-shipped. And wait… the sales order for 1000 products had a larger total? Why isn't that on here? And… where's our cash? Shouldn't we have some cash from that order?

Did we forget something…? …We never sent an invoice. And without an invoice, we never received payment from our customer.

Let's create the invoice. Leave this ad-hoc Financial Statement screen up. We'll come back to it throughout this lab. Create a new session.

Invoicing the Customer

Transaction Code: VF04

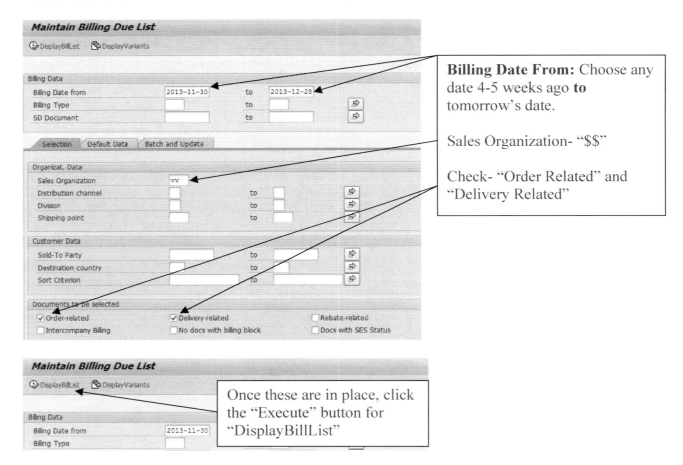

Billing Date From: Choose any date 4-5 weeks ago **to** tomorrow's date.

Sales Organization- "$$"

Check- "Order Related" and "Delivery Related"

Once these are in place, click the "Execute" button for "DisplayBillList"

You may have more than one billing document here—remember that your group is also completing these labs and may be ahead of or behind you. If there is more than one billing document, use the document which corresponds with your "Outbound Delivery" number from SAP Lab 02. (Use the *Relevant Information* form at the end of this supplemental text.)

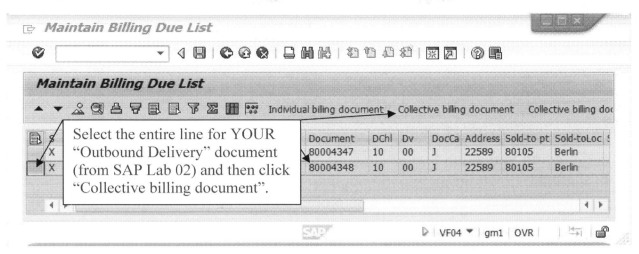

Select the entire line for YOUR "Outbound Delivery" document (from SAP Lab 02) and then click "Collective billing document".

It doesn't look like anything has happened, but an invoice has been created. And you need that invoice number to complete the next step.

Select the entire line for your "Outbound Delivery" document again. Under the heading "Environment", click "Display document."

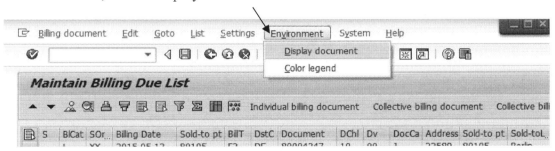

Your "Outbound Delivery" Document, from SAP Lab 02, will appear. Choose the header "Environment" and then click on "Document Flow".

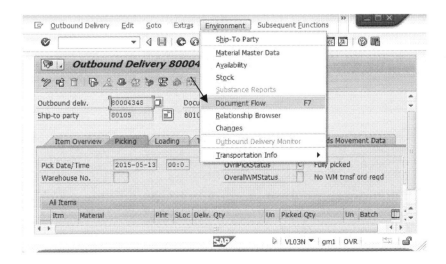

The next screen shows the updated "Document flow" since SAP Lab 02.

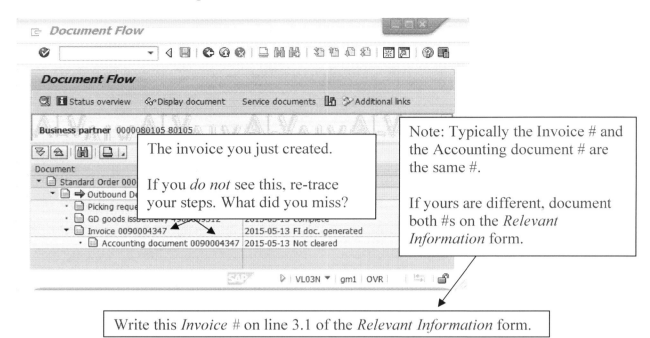

Note: Typically the Invoice # and the Accounting document # are the same #.

If yours are different, document both #s on the *Relevant Information* form.

The invoice you just created.

If you *do not* see this, re-trace your steps. What did you miss?

Write this *Invoice* # on line 3.1 of the *Relevant Information* form.

In addition, we can see how this transaction has affected our company's financials. Switch over to your Financial Statements session (F.01).

There isn't a "refresh" button for this screen, so you'll have to back out and go back in. Use the same parameters as last time. When you come back in, what do you see?

> **Note: Remember that your numbers WILL be different. Your total sale and cost of raw materials are different—and the rest of your group is interacting within this same company. You should, however, see a difference when you return to this screen.

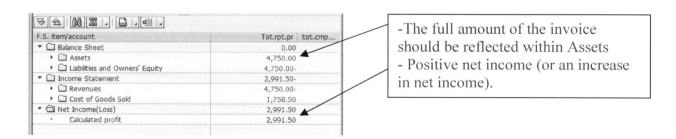

-The full amount of the invoice should be reflected within Assets
- Positive net income (or an increase in net income).

But, wait—why did net income increase, but we've never received payment?

ERPsim runs accrual basis accounting, not cash basis accounting. All we need is a promise of payment and it counts as revenue. At the same time, note that we still haven't *paid* for our raw

materials. With accrual based accounting, cash is secondary to the documentation itself. An invoiced sales order counts as revenue. An invoice for raw materials counts as a liability.

Let's continue with every organization's dream—and receive payment for our sales order before we pay for the raw materials.

Switch back to your other session, and return to the main SAP menu.

Receive Payment from the Customer

Transaction Code: F-28

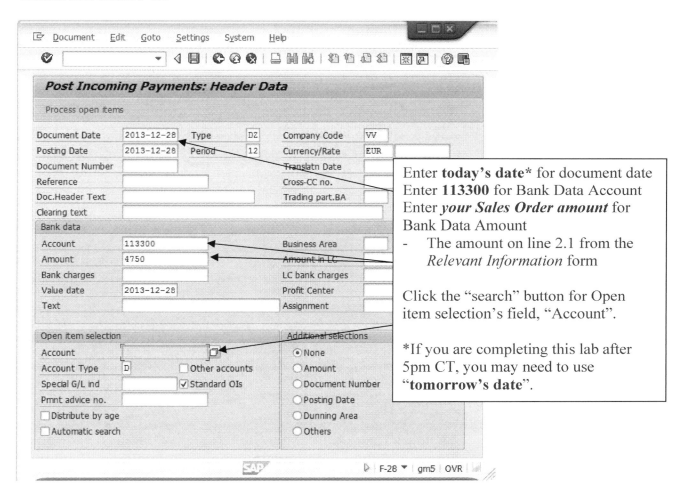

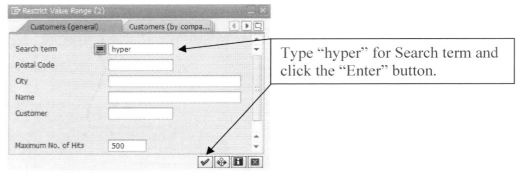

Type "hyper" for Search term and click the "Enter" button.

Do you remember who you sold to? The screen shots were the Hypermarket in Berlin. Did you sell to them? If not, figure out who you sold to and choose them.

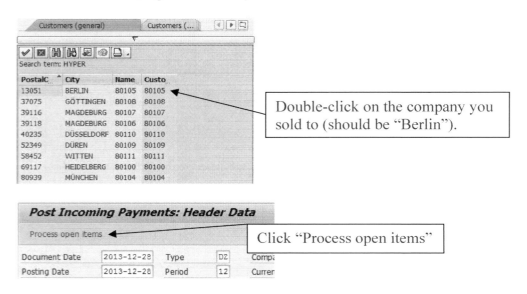

Double-click on the company you sold to (should be "Berlin").

Click "Process open items"

Slow down as you move into the next screen.

This is bookkeeping. The person who would typically be using these transactions will spend all day buzzing around between a few of these transactions.

You are not the bookkeeper for this company. You are likely unfamiliar with these SAP transactions. SAP assumes that you know what you're doing here, and will give limited feedback as you click around. This is not intuitive.

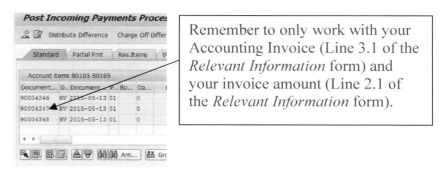

Remember to only work with your Accounting Invoice (Line 3.1 of the *Relevant Information* form) and your invoice amount (Line 2.1 of the *Relevant Information* form).

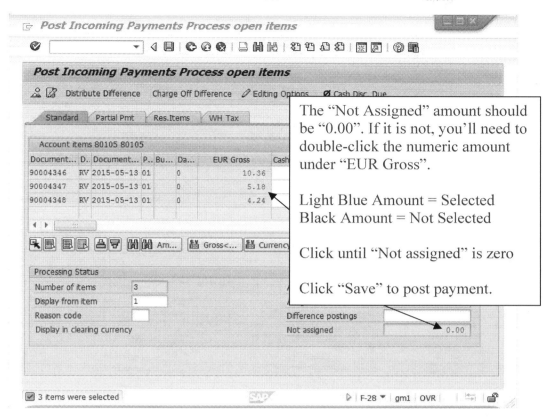

Click back to the SAP menu—if you are given the message "Data will be lost", choose "Yes" to exit editing.

Now, click back to your Financial Statement session. Back out and go back in to make the data current. What do you see? Anything different?

Think about this—your cash account reflects your Sales Order's Total Value, but you have positive net income. You've never paid for the raw materials—why isn't your net income the same as your cash account?

Remember, ERPsim uses accrual basis accounting. You may have cash in your account, but you still owe for those raw materials. Let's set this right. Did you ever receive invoices for your raw materials?

Switch back to the other session. Click the Back button until you return to the SAP Menu.

Lab 03 – Accounting and Bookkeeping

Enter Incoming Invoice

Transaction Code: MIRO

Remember that you purchased raw materials from two different organizations. One PO went to a food vendor, FOODBROKER'S INC. The other PO went to CONTINENTAL PRINTING. You'll have to receive and pay two different invoices.

Let's start with FOODBROKER'S Inc.

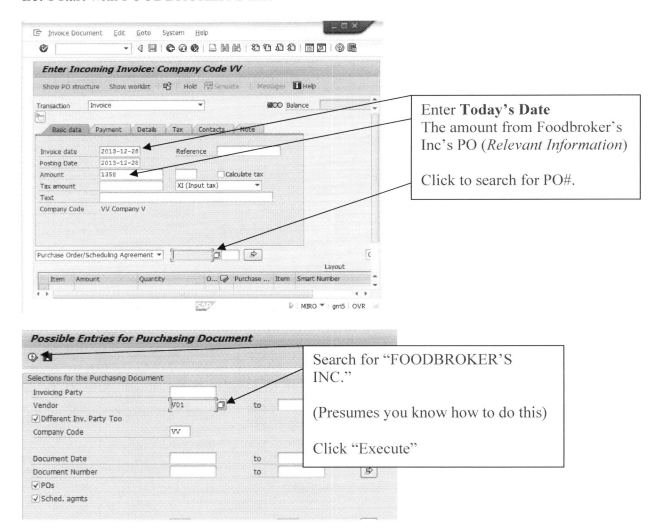

Depending on where your group members are in this lab, you may see a list of available PO Numbers. Work ONLY with your PO Number, not your entire group's POs

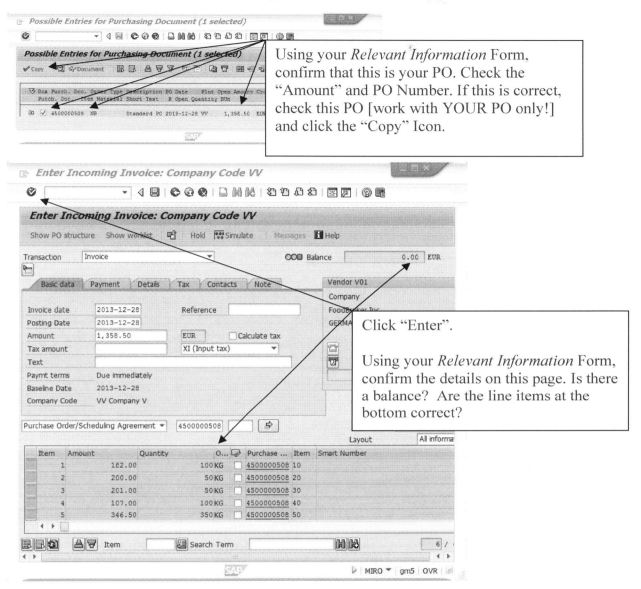

Using your *Relevant Information* Form, confirm that this is your PO. Check the "Amount" and PO Number. If this is correct, check this PO [work with YOUR PO only!] and click the "Copy" Icon.

Click "Enter".

Using your *Relevant Information* Form, confirm the details on this page. Is there a balance? Are the line items at the bottom correct?

Now click the simulate button (Simulate), which will bring up the following screen:

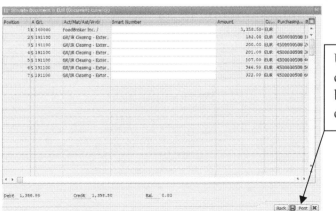

Using your *Relevant Information* Form, confirm these details one more time. Is there a balance? Are the line items at the bottom correct? If everything is correct, click "Post".

Received the error "Blocked for Payment"? This error typically comes from an information mismatch between the "amount" entered, the vendor, or sometimes the date. Check your information. If everything is entered correctly, click "save". Often it just works!

If you do not receive an error, click back to the SAP Menu.

Post Outgoing Payment

Transaction Code: F-53

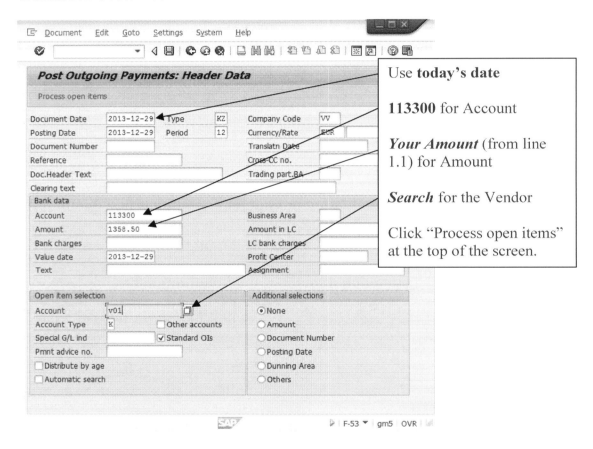

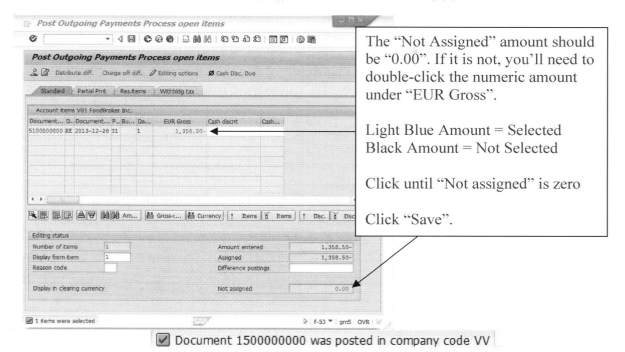

The "Not Assigned" amount should be "0.00". If it is not, you'll need to double-click the numeric amount under "EUR Gross".

Light Blue Amount = Selected
Black Amount = Not Selected

Click until "Not assigned" is zero

Click "Save".

Document 1500000000 was posted in company code VV

Back out of this screen, answering "Yes" to the following question:

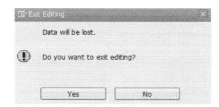

Now switch back to your Financial Statement session. Back out and go back in to refresh the data.

Notice that, while your net income has stayed the same (depending on what your group members are doing, of course), the assets have changed. Open the tree to see what's listed under your cash account and current liabilities.

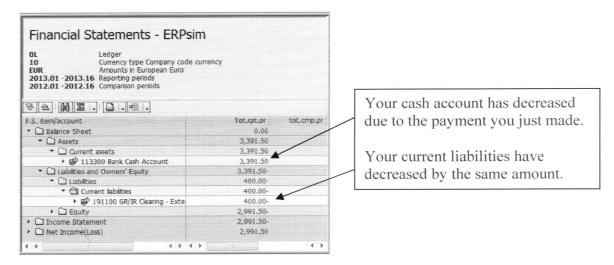

Your cash account has decreased due to the payment you just made.

Your current liabilities have decreased by the same amount.

Now let's go back and finish up the remaining Current liabilities. Repeat the previous steps to complete the payment for Continental Printing.

Switch back to your other session. Click the "Back" button until you've returned to the SAP Menu.

Enter Incoming Invoice

Transaction Code: MIRO

Remember that you purchased raw materials from two different organizations. One PO went to a food vendor, FOODBROKER'S INC. The other PO went to CONTINENTAL PRINTING. You'll have to receive and pay two different invoices.

Let's finish this section of our accounting lab by processing Continental Printing's invoice.

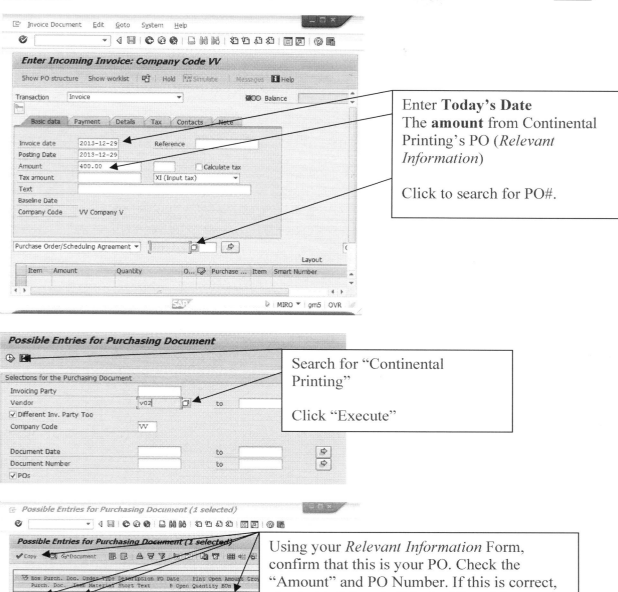

Enter **Today's Date**
The **amount** from Continental Printing's PO (*Relevant Information*)

Click to search for PO#.

Search for "Continental Printing"

Click "Execute"

Using your *Relevant Information* Form, confirm that this is your PO. Check the "Amount" and PO Number. If this is correct, check this PO and click the "Copy" Icon.

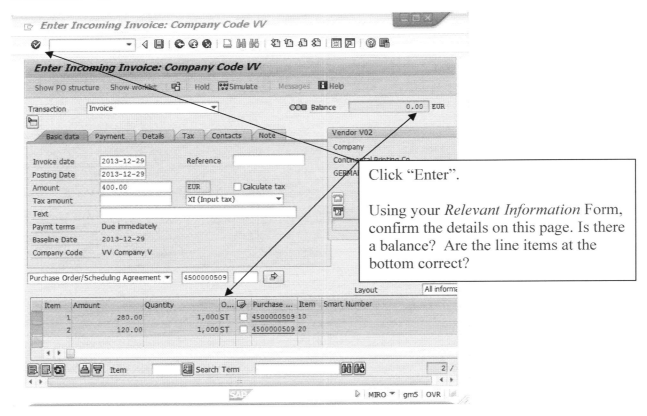

Now click the simulate button ( ). (If simulate is not available, confirm your amounts and click the Save/Post button).

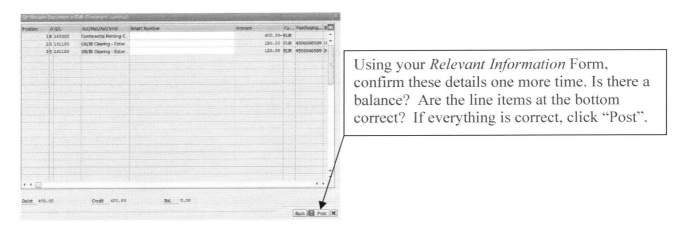

Received the error "Blocked for Payment"? This error typically comes from an information mismatch between the "amount" entered, the vendor, or sometimes the date. Check your information. If everything is entered correctly, click "save". Often it just works!

Click back to the SAP Menu.

Post Outgoing Payment

Transaction Code: F-53

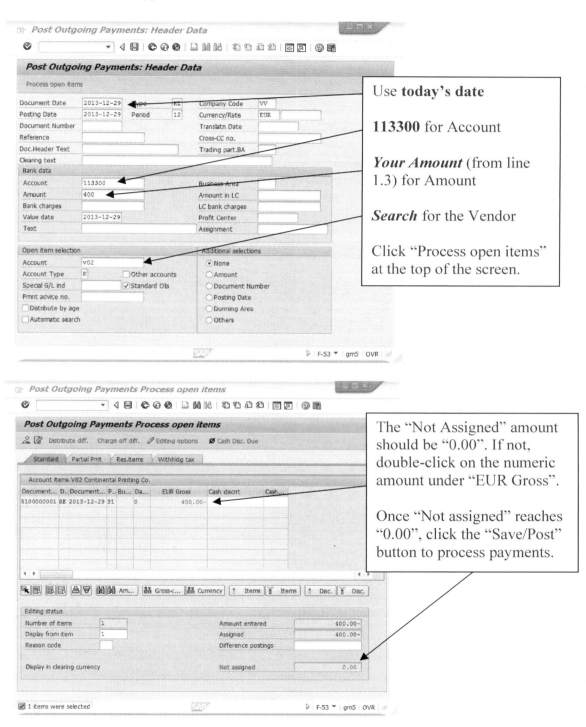

Click back to the SAP Menu. Click yes to the following message:

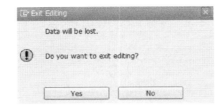

Now switch back to your Financial Statement session. Back out and go back in to refresh the data.

Notice that, while your net income has stayed the same (depending on what your group members are doing, of course), the assets have changed. Open the tree to see what's listed under your cash account and current liabilities.

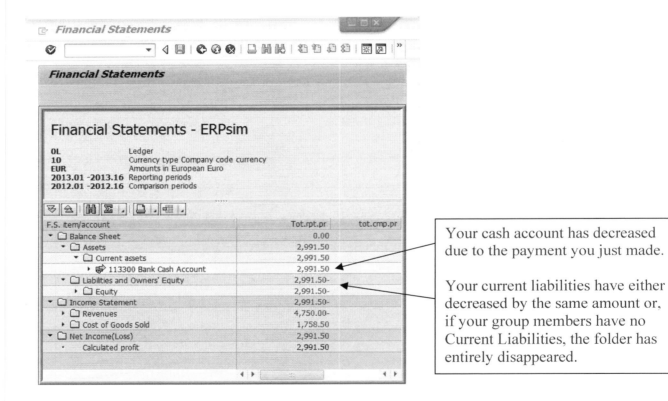

Your cash account has decreased due to the payment you just made.

Your current liabilities have either decreased by the same amount or, if your group members have no Current Liabilities, the folder has entirely disappeared.

Invest in your company

The final transaction to complete will be to reinvest your available cash back into your company. There are two options for reinvestment within ERPsim.

> One option is to **decrease set up time** between products. The default set up time is 12 hours, which means that every time you switch your production line from one product to another, you lose half of one day's total production (12 of the available 24 hours). If your group's strategy is to focus on one or two products, reduction of set up time may not make much of a difference. If you plan to switch between all six products, set up time reduction could make a tremendous difference within your production efficiency.

> The other option is to **increase the capacity** of your production line. The default capacity is 21,000 products per day. Remember that 21,000 per day is –after—set up time between products. Depending on your strategy, increased capacity may make more of an impact on your production.

> Or, any combination of the above two.

From the ERPsim Extended Manufacturing job aid, here are some milestones with their corresponding investment amount:

Production Improvements

SETUP TIME OPTIONS	
Setup time* (hours)	Investment** (€)
12h00	-
10h00	62 500
8h00	167 000
5h20	500 000
4h00	1 000 000

ADDITIONAL CAPACITY above 24,000 boxes per day	
Additional capacity	Investment** (€)
1,000	1 000 000
2,000	2 000 000
...	...
9,000	9 000 000
10,000	10 000 000

Within this lab, <u>you'll invest cash to increase your capacity</u>. To start, determine your available cash—specifically based on your product's sales.

Turn to the *Relevant Information* form at the end of the textbook.

Take the total from your Sales Order (line 2.1) and subtract the total cost of your Raw Materials (line 1.1 + line 1.3). The remaining balance is your available cash.

$$2.1 - (1.1+1.3)$$

Sales Order – Total Raw Material Cost

= Available Cash for Reinvestment

Write this total down on line 3.2 on the *Relevant Information* form.

Switch from your Financial Statement session to the other session. Click the Back button until you reach the SAP Menu. Click through any messages asking you to save.

Transaction Code: FB50

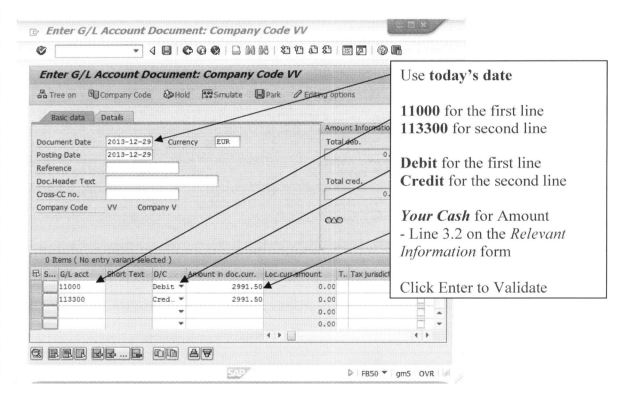

Upon validation (clicking Enter), the common database will be queried. Notice the accounts you're using here. 11000 is the G/L account for "Machinery and equip.".

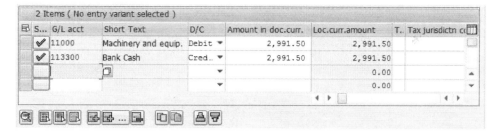

If there are no errors, click "Save" to post this transaction.

☑ Document 100000000 was posted in company code VV

Switch back to your Financial Statement session.

Back out and go back in to "refresh" the statement.

At first glance, it looks like nothing has changed. But, if you expand the folders you'll see the assets have been re-arranged. Your cash is no longer within the "Cash Account", but is now listed under "Long-term Assets". Specifically, "011000 Machinery and equipment".

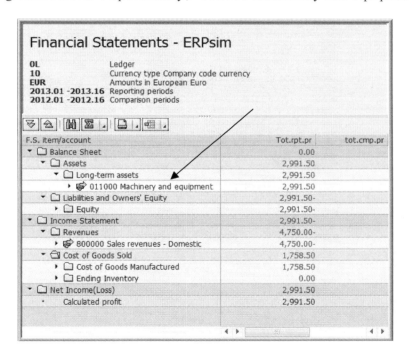

Expand the Long-term assets, Liabilities and Owner's Equity, Revenues, and Cost of Goods Sold trees. Use your (print screen) key on your keyboard to copy your Financial Statements. Open MS Word and paste the screen shot into the word file.

Submit this Word file into your LMT (D2L, Blackboard, Canvas, etc.) under the "Lab 03" assignment.

Save the file as:

"Last_Name - $# - Lab 03" (i.e., "Rutherford – V6 - Lab 03")

Make a note of where you are saving your file.

If you are using computer lab: if you log off or are logged off for inactivity before uploading this file, you may lose the file.

Upload this file to your LMT under the LABS / LAB 03 assignment.

No printed copies will be accepted.

Part II

Supplemental Readings

Section 01 - What is ERP?

ERP is "*Enterprise Resource Planning*". "ERP", within this course, refers to a single software system utilized by an entire organization to manage all aspects of the organization. This software isn't productivity software (like a word processor or spreadsheet) but the software that runs an organization.

A well-integrated ERP system manages all functional areas: Sales/Marketing, Operations and Supply Chain Management (OSCM), Accounting/Finance, and Human Resources (HR). This allows everyone from an entry-level Customer Service Representative (CSR) up to the C-Level executives to have real-time access to all necessary and relevant information that is of value to their role within the organization.

This complete data integration allows for more accurate and timely information, which helps managers more quickly and more accurately make decisions for the organizations. In addition, this information makes each individual's tasks more efficient as they have access to relevant information from all functional areas—right there in the single ERP system.

As a result of this single ERP system, decision making—and—customer service improves. With a well-integrated ERP system, the entire organization becomes more efficient, and more profitable.

What If An Organization Doesn't Have ERP?

The good news is that an organization without ERP is not doomed to failure. There are many successful organizations without a single ERP software package. However, an argument could be made that all organizations would benefit from a well-integrated all-encompassing single ERP system.

ERP in Action: How Customers Benefit from ERP

Using a CSR (Customer Service Representative) as an example, presume that a customer calls to place an order. That customer will likely want to know if the product they are purchasing is in-stock, and how quickly the product will be shipped. If the customer has a line-of-credit with the company, they may want information on their available credit. Without one common ERP software package across the organization, the CSR may not have this information available in "real-time".

CSR Example – Taking an Order Within an ERP System.

Taking this scenario to its fullest—what if the customer calls and needs to order a specific quantity of finished goods? They'll want to know the exact price for that quantity and if it's

available in stock. Just to make it more complicated, they need to know the exact weight for the total shipped package.

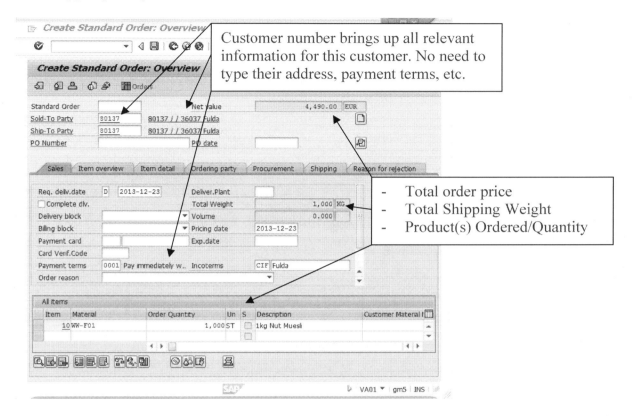

Within the SAP Sales Order screen, the CSR has access to company-wide information that is relevant to the customer's order.

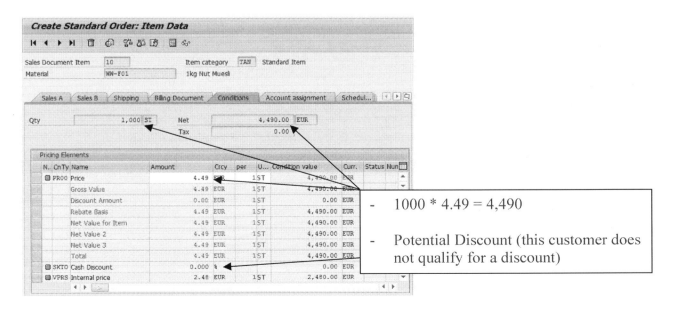

At the click of a button, the CSR can see how the order's price was determined. For this order, the price is simply Quantity 1000 * 4.49, the standard price for this product. This pricing is set by another department—perhaps marketing, perhaps a sales team. The CSR does not need to know *who* created the pricing structure, but simply what the price is and how it was calculated.

While on the phone with the customer, the CSR can also check the product's stock. No need to call the warehouse, or access a separate system, just click a button. This is referred to as "Available to Promise" or ATP.

Depending on how the ERP system is configured, the CSR may only see what is available in stock, or they may see the production orders with estimates of when the product will be available. This information is important as the CSR will be able to tell the customer when they can expect shipment of their order.

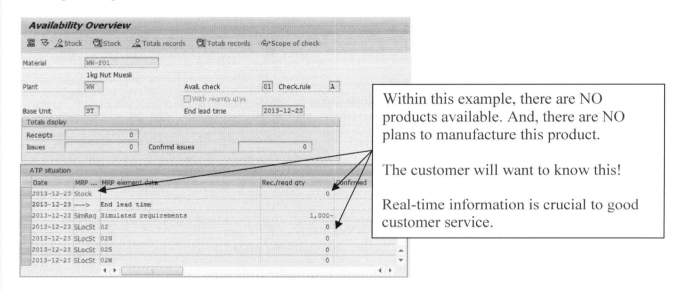

For more details, the sales order process is completed within SAP Lab 02.

What is it About ERP That Makes Information Available in "Real-Time"?

A well implemented ERP system incorporates all functional areas within a company. Information from one area, one department, one employee, is available to all other areas, departments, and employees who would benefit from the information. This information becomes available across the organization due to ERP using a common database, or collection of data. One ERP system, or software package, with a *common database* allows all relevant information from all areas of the organization to be available to all areas of the organization that may need it.

Why is ERP Integral to a Successful Strategy?

Simply: decision making and customer service.

There are two overall strategies within any organization:

Low-Cost – Having the lowest-priced product or service on the market. Generally, this strategy involves finding a commodity item, standardizing it, procuring the lowest-cost raw materials, the least expensive labor, and/or the most cost-effective means of distribution. Ultimately, this strategy offers a product or service that meets the needs of most individuals, with the lowest price on the market.

Personalized / Customized – Having a product or service that fits exactly what the customer wants. Most times this personalized / customized product or service is *not* the least expensive product on the market. It's, generally, a made-to-order product or service following the customer's specifications or requirements.

Of course, somewhere in-between is where most organizations find themselves: somewhat customized, at a reasonable price. Both are customer-oriented. Both require nimble decision making.

A common database helps to successfully (profitably) execute either strategy.

If there is lag-time between the transfer of information, processes are less efficient. A well implemented organization-wide ERP system allows for all relevant information to be easily accessible, which ultimately makes processes more efficient, and improves the customer's experience. And that's the ultimate goal within an organization—an improved customer experience.

A happy customer makes for a more profitable organization.

Future Sections

A handful of popular ERP systems include: Microsoft Dynamics, Oracle, UNIT4, Global Shop, OpenPRO, and SAP. This textbook focuses entirely on SAP's R/3 ERP system.

As an example throughout, we will use ERPsim Muesli, a fictitious manufacturing company, as an example organization utilizing ERP as a strategy. While this manufacturer is far too small and simple to warrant the full SAP R/3 system, the simplicity of this fictitious company makes understanding of ERP, and SAP, easier.

Whenever possible, future sections will discuss "real world" scenarios, but it will largely focus on playing the ERPsim Manufacturing Game.

Section 02 - Sales Forecast

What is a Sales Forecast?

It's, quite simply, how much a company plans to sell within a given time period.

Every manufacturer requires a sales forecast. Period. This forecast is what puts everything into place; everything into motion. Without it, how does a company know how many of each product to manufacture? How do purchasing agents know which and how many raw materials to purchase? How do sales managers put together realistic sales quotas? How does a controller know if company goals are being met? The sales forecast is at the base of every manufacturing company's decisions. Operations, Supply Chain, Sales, Marketing… it all starts with the sales forecast.

Within the "real world", this is referred to as S&OP, or "Sales and Operations Planning". S&OP can be very complicated and often requires extensive research, statistical models, and many other factors. Within the ERPsim Manufacturing Game, the parameters are much simpler.

Within this section we'll calculate a starting forecast specific to the Manufacturing Game.

The Reality of a Sales Forecast

Like with "real world" S&OP, if there were a guaranteed way to create an accurate sales forecast, every company would create and/or manufacture exactly the number of products to meet customer demand at any given time. In that reality tells us that this is impossible (companies routinely produce too many or too few products), we have to accept that our sales forecast is a "guess". However, we try to create as educated of a "guess" as possible.

Creating an "Educated Guess" for our Initial Sales Forecast

While the next section details a calculation for your Muesli company's initial forecast, it's merely an educated guess—a starting point. As you learn more about the simulation, your company, and determine a winning strategy, your initial forecast will undoubtedly change. And, as you'll find, even with ERPsim's simplicity, there will be no *perfect* sales forecast.

To start, you'll want to determine how many products you think you could (or should) sell within a day. Product sales relies on other factors (pricing, product, marketing, etc), but for production, you'll want to assume that you'll sell everything you manufacture within a day. Again, how to actually and consistently sell these products is another topic. Within this section, in creating our initial sales forecast, we'll presume to sell the same number of products as we manufacture within any given simulated day.

In order to calculate the number of products your company can produce within a day, you'll need to determine and understand your company's production capabilities and limitations.

The Manufacturing Game simulates a 24-hour day with possible production taking place across the full 24-hours. Without production upgrades, the initial production capacity is 1000 products per hour, or 24,000 finished products across 24 hours/one day. This capacity continues at 24,000 per simulated day until another product is scheduled for production. Each time production shifts to a new product, there is mandatory set-up time. Without investment in set-up time reduction, the initial set-up time between products is 12 hours, or half of one day's production (12 of the available 24 hours).

Without production improvements:

Daily Production Capacity: **24,000** Finished Goods (boxes of muesli—any size, any recipe)

Set-up time between products: **12** hours, or half of one day's production

Depending on the length of the scheduled production run, your company's daily production capacity will be somewhere between 12,000 (1000 * 12 hours) and 24,000 (1000 * 24 hours) per day.

Getting back to your daily sales—how many finished goods can you manufacture within a day? As a "guess", consider an average of the minimum and maximum production per day:

Minimum = 12,000   Maximum = 24,000

Average = **18,000** finished products per 24 hour day

Based on this average, you would presume to sell 18,000 finished goods per day. This is your average daily production.

But, let's take this a step further. Your company is capable of manufacturing six products. It is your goal to, at any given time, have all six products in stock and available for sale. With a good market price and reasonable marketing, you'll be spreading your average daily sales across all six products.

Take the average daily sale and divide it among the 6 products:

18,000 (total products sold) / 6 (total products) = 3,000 (individual finished goods sold per day)

For Product One, you presume to sell 3,000 each day. Product Two, 3,000. Product Three, etc. etc.

However, your product requires raw materials and those raw materials must be ordered from a vendor. Within the ERPsim Manufacturing Game, lead-time for receiving delivery of raw materials is 3-5 days. Once the materials are in-stock, with 6 products and an average of 18,000 products manufactured per day, it may be 6 days before a product is even produced (producing one product per day, six products, six days).

How many days between ordering raw materials and production of the sixth product?

Lead-time = 3-5 days   Production = 1-6 days

5 (max lead-time) + 6 (max production [total products])

Maximum Days to Product availability = (5 + 6) = 11

Simulated Day:	1-5	6	7	8	9	10	11
Daily Action:	Raw Material Lead Time	Product One	Product Two	Product Three	Product Four	Product Five	Product Six

The initial "educated guess" sales forecast within the ERPsim Extended Manufacturing Game is:

11 (max. days to produce) * 3,000 (expected per-product sales per day) = **33,000**

Recapping the calculation:

Daily production capacity is 24,000 with setup time between products of 12 hours or ½ of daily production (12 of the 24 available hours). The minimum production per day is 12,000 and maximum is 24,000. Your average daily production is 18,000.

((Max Capacity) + (Max Capacity * (1-(setup time / 24)))) / 2

((24,000) + (24,000 * (1-(12/24)))) / 2

= 18,000 Average Products Sold Per Day

- -

(Average Products Sold Per Day) / (Total Number of Products to Manufacture)

(18,000 / 6)

= 3,000 (Individual Finished Goods Sold Per Day)

- -

Finished Goods Sold Per Day * (Max Lead Time + Total Number of Products to Manufacture)
3,000 * (5 + 6)

= **33,000** Starting per Product Sales Forecast

Like a sales forecast within the "real world", there are no guarantees that this is what you will sell. It is an educated guess based on our limitations and a "best case" sales scenario.

It will, undoubtedly, need to be adjusted as you acquire additional information.

Why Would You Change Your Sales Forecast?

The only reason you would change your forecast is because your "educated guess" has become "better educated". You had to start somewhere. But, if you forecast for too much, you may have production bogged down on a product that isn't selling while you've run out of a product that is selling. Or, the opposite, if you forecast for too few of a product—below customer demand—you may find yourself constantly out-of-stock of the product. Both of these result in not having products available for sale, or a stock out. If you have frequent stock outs, you're losing revenue, and it is unlikely that you will be profitable.

Examples of why you'd change your forecast:

- Perhaps you've found that no matter what you do, you just can't sell one or two products. Maybe you'll choose to limit production of those products? Or, perhaps you'll stop producing them all-together.

- Perhaps you've found that you can't keep certain products on your shelves—and you're selling them at a profitable margin. If this is the case, you may choose to focus your production on those products and increase those products' forecast.

- You've increased your production capacity, or decreased set-up time, or reduced/increased the number of products you're manufacturing.

- Any combination of the above, or something else entirely. This is, after all, just a series of guesses. Hopefully educated guesses.

As you gain more experience within the ERPsim Manufacturing Game, you will find that your per-product forecast will vary. In addition, each ERPsim game is complete with a whole new market—with varying product preferences. It is unlikely that you'll keep the same forecast for all 6 products throughout each game, or from game-to-game.

Don't Change Your Forecast Too Often, or Too Quickly!

You'll want to gauge the market over a period of time. Remember that you're making "educated" guesses, and those guesses become more accurate with more information. Making quick decisions from day-to-day may leave you with inaccurate information—how do you know for sure that what you saw during one or a few days isn't the result of another team's poor playing?

Remember that you're competing with other teams selling the same product, within the same market. One team may manufacture 100,000 of a particular product, set their price below everyone else, and then sell out within 2-3 days. They have the same limitations as you—they can only produce about 24,000 per day. They are also limited by 6-11 days' worth of

manufacturing lead-time. If they sell all 100,000 of their products within 2-3 days, they may steal market share for a few days, but then they will have a stock-out for the next 6-10 days leaving your product the only one available for sale. You notice a drop in sales and then your sales go back up to normal.

The following graph shows the total sales for one product across 7 competing teams.

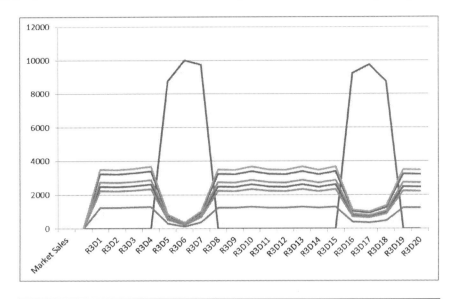

| Why did your sales drop? When should you make a decision? |

As you can see, 6 of the teams show steady sales of this product, while one company shows completely erratic and inconsistent sales, oscillating between selling nothing and out-selling every other team.

As one of the 6 teams with steady sales, you have no idea what is happening with that 7th team. All you see is your team's sales—steady, steady, DROP, steady, steady, steady, DROP, steady.

If you make quick decisions regarding your sales, you may miss what's really going on.

Within the next graph, on Round 3, Day 6 (R3D6) sales have dropped dramatically. What do you do? Drop your price? Increase marketing? Or, wait and see what's really going on? Perhaps, as you can see with this overall market report, one team doesn't know what they're doing and are out-selling everyone for a limited time. If you make a quick decision, what happens next?

The following graph illustrates what may happen with a quick reaction:

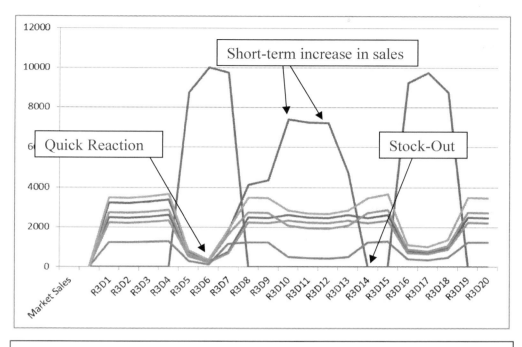

A quick reaction may boost sales in the short-term, but ends in a stock-out.

As you can see, the inexperienced team has created a great deal of product, priced it too low, and out-sold the market (which creates a drop in sales for all other teams). One of the seven teams makes a knee-jerk decision to lower their price, which results in a dramatic increase in sales, followed by a stock-out—they were unprepared for an increase in sales. A stock-out **rarely** leads to an increase in profits.

For the most part, making quick decisions may not help the longevity and long term profitability of your company. If something is working—and abruptly stops working—there may be other factors involved.

Educated Guess

Just remember that your initial sales forecast is always going to be a guess. However, there are ways to make your guess as educated as possible. Within the "real world", you'll want to research the market and make an educated guess. Within the ERPsim Manufacturing Game, you can start with an educated guess based on your capacity, set-up time, and lead-time. This forecast will need to be updated as the simulation continues, you gain additional information (through the provided reports), or you make changes to your infrastructure.

Creating a Sales Forecast in ERPsim's Manufacturing Game

Transaction Code: MD61

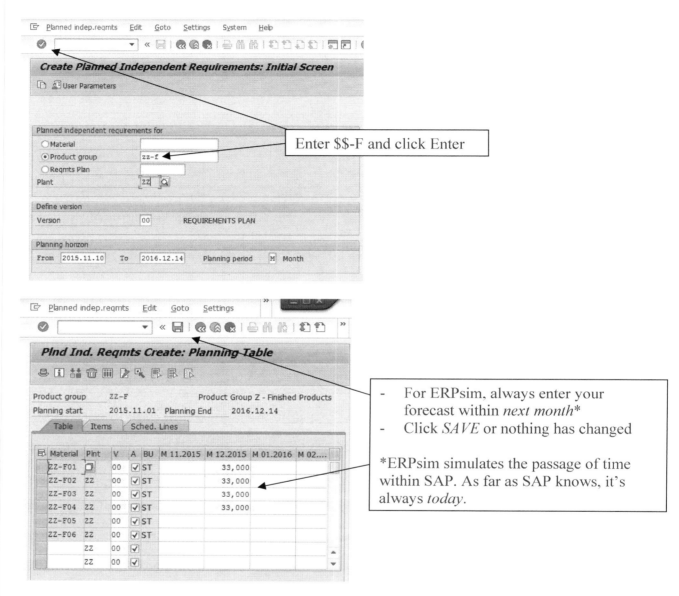

Enter $$-F and click Enter

- For ERPsim, always enter your forecast within *next month**
- Click *SAVE* or nothing has changed

*ERPsim simulates the passage of time within SAP. As far as SAP knows, it's always *today*.

Enter your forecast within *next month*, then click "save" (💾) and the 🏠 button to return to the SAP menu.

Note—*Next Month*

ERPsim's simulation software is "spoofing" the system. To the actual SAP servers, the date is always today. Your forecast needs to be in "next month" which is the next calendar month relative to *today's date*. Whether it's the first day of the actual month or the last day of the actual month, next month is always the next calendar month. Remember, the simulation is simulating

the passage of time. The simulated day and round is not relevant to today's actual date, next month is always "next Month".

Goal of a Sales Forecast within ERPsim

Within ERPsim, your goal is to sell *about* what you can produce within a day. If you're producing *about* what you sell within a day—at a profitable price—you're likely to increase your net income.

How does a forecast fit into production? The next step is MRP.

Section 03 - MRP

What is MRP?

MRP is "Material Requirements Planning". It is nothing more than planning. You can run MRP all day, but all you'll do is create a new plan. Nothing is ordered, nothing is produced. MRP is planning.

What does MRP *plan*?

MRP plans for production. MRP looks at your sales forecast, looks at the raw material inventory, the finished goods inventory, and goods in production, and then calculates a *plan* to manufacture enough products to meet your sales forecast.

This plan includes two different parts: *planned purchase orders* and *planned production*.

Planned Purchase Orders

Purchase Orders (POs) are the official documents companies utilize to authorize the order of raw materials, supplies, services, and other company expenses. These purchase orders document how much was purchased, which department authorized the purchase, which "cost center" is responsible for the expense, and anything else the company might require to accompany the purchase of –anything– from an outside vendor.

Running MRP creates the *plan* to purchase raw materials required for manufacturing various finished goods. Within SAP, *planned* purchase orders are called *Purchase Requisitions*. Purchase Requisitions are unauthorized, planned, or suggested *Purchase Orders*. Creating purchase requisitions is nothing but planning.

Just like in the "real world", planned purchase orders, or purchase requisitions, must be converted into *Purchase Orders* to officially authorize and order the raw materials.

Planned Production Orders

Production Orders instruct a manufacturing company on which products to produce, and how many of those products to produce.

Within SAP's MRP process, instead of creating production orders directly, *planned production orders* are created. Nothing is scheduled to be produced—this is the product *plan* based on the sales forecast and current inventory and production levels.

Once raw materials have been delivered, these planned orders can be converted into actual *Production Orders*. Nothing is manufactured and nothing is produced until these planned orders are converted into *Production Orders.*

Remember this about MRP:

MRP is planning. Nothing happens when you run MRP—except a plan is generated.

If you run MRP multiple times, it removes the previous "plan" and creates a new "plan" based on the current conditions.

"Open" Purchase Requisitions (those that haven't been converted to Purchase Orders) are "closed" and then replaced by new "open" Purchase Requisitions. Planned Production Orders which have not been converted are also replaced by new Planned Production Orders.

MRP always creates a new set of plans based on current conditions

How does MRP Know What to Order?

Before MRP is run, SAP needs to know the sales forecast for each product and the required raw materials within each manufactured product. This information is set within the Bill of Materials, or BOM.

Within ERPsim, you can see the BOM for any of the products.

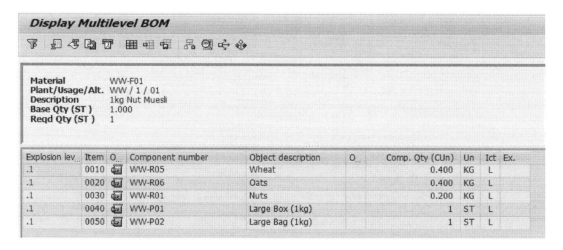

These are the listed components for the 1kg Nut Muesli product. The final product is a 1kg box of Nut Muesli cereal. The total food materials must equal 1kg in weight: 0.4kg Wheat, 0.4kg Oats, and 0.2kg of Nuts = 1kg. In addition, you'll see that each product requires 1 (appropriately sized) box, and 1 (appropriately sized) bag. For the 1kg product, one large box and one large bag are required within the BOM.

> **ERPsim Specific**—Within ERPsim, the time-frame for the sales forecast is from MRP run to MRP run, not round to round nor day to day. ERPsim is spoofing the system into seeing the passage of time, but within SAP, it's always today. While the sales forecast is entered into "next month", ERPsim uses that quantity each time MRP is run.
>
> Don't mistake the sales forecast for "total sales within a round". It is total sales from MRP run to MRP run.

Running MRP

We have our sales forecast (from Section 2), we have the BOM. Now what?

Within SAP, and specifically within the ERPsim Manufacturing Game, you run through one SAP transaction and MRP has been run. The transaction is simple, but a lot happens when you run this transaction.

Moving forward from Section 2, Sales Forecast, let's run through the process of MRP the very first time you run MRP within the ERPsim Manufacturing Game. We'll start with our initial forecast of 33,000 and specifically track $$-F01, 1kg Nut Muesli.

The MRP Process – How is it Calculated?

Using the BOM for 1kg Nut Muesli, MRP calculates the number of raw materials necessary to meet your sales forecast. MRP looks at your sales forecast and then compares it to your current inventory/stock levels for that finished product:

SLoc	Material	Material Description	Stock	Unit
02	WW-F01	1kg Nut Muesli	0	ST
	WW-F02	1kg Blueberry Muesli	0	ST
	WW-F03	1kg Strawberry Muesli	0	ST
	WW-F04	1kg Raisin Muesli	0	ST
	WW-F05	1kg Original Muesli	0	ST
	WW-F06	1kg Mixed Fruit Muesli	0	ST

Inventory Report: Round 1 Day 01

At the start of the simulation, your inventory is ZERO for all finished goods. You also have nothing scheduled for production, so the production numbers do not factor into the calculation.

Using 33,000 as the forecast, MRP calculates that all 33,000 of the sales forecast must be manufactured for this finished product.

From here, MRP looks to your current raw material inventory for its current stock. MRP will calculate and *plan* to order only enough raw materials to create 33,000 1kg Nut Muesli.

The BOM tells MRP which raw materials are required for this finished product:

Item	ICt	Component	Component description	Quantity	Un
0010	L	WW-R05	Wheat	0.400	KG
0020	L	WW-R06	Oats	0.400	KG
0030	L	WW-R01	Nuts	0.200	KG
0040	L	WW-P01	Large Box (1kg)	1	ST
0050	L	WW-P02	Large Bag (1kg)	1	ST

For each of the listed raw materials, MRP will then calculate the quantity of each raw material to purchase. In order to do this, MRP looks at the current raw material inventory:

88	WW-P01	Large Box (1kg)	0	ST
	WW-P02	Large Bag (1kg)	0	ST
	WW-P03	Small Box (500g)	0	ST
	WW-P04	Small Bag (500g)	0	ST
	WW-R01	Nuts	0	KG
	WW-R02	Blueberries	0	KG
	WW-R03	Strawberries	0	KG
	WW-R04	Raisins	0	KG
	WW-R05	Wheat	0	KG
	WW-R06	Oats	0	KG

Because the simulation has just started, there is no raw material inventory in stock. MRP must calculate for the purchase of all required raw materials to match the initial sales forecast.

Once the calculations are complete, MRP creates a *purchase requisition*, a planned purchase order, for each of the raw materials:

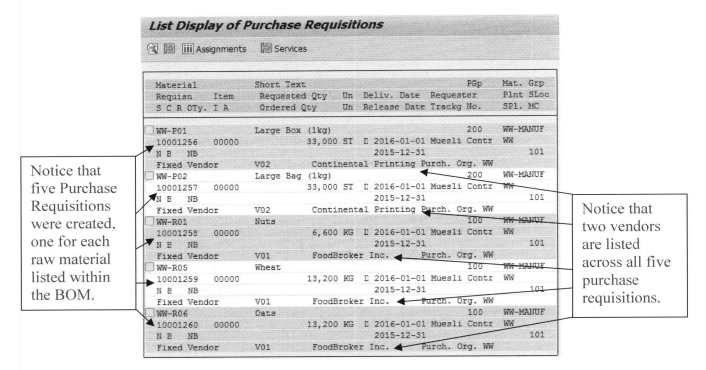

Notice that five Purchase Requisitions were created, one for each raw material listed within the BOM.

Notice that two vendors are listed across all five purchase requisitions.

Within the above purchase requisitions, you can see the quantity for each raw material. Why does it list 33,000 boxes and bags, but far fewer of the other three raw materials?

Look at the BOM. Note that each finished product requires one box and one bag, but the food raw materials are a percentage of 1kg. Purchases of food raw materials are in quantities of 1 full kilogram of each product. Your BOM, the recipe for the finished good, lists a percentage of the raw material. While your forecast is for 33,000 finished goods, you need to order fewer food raw materials to complete those finished goods. For 1kg Nut Muesli:

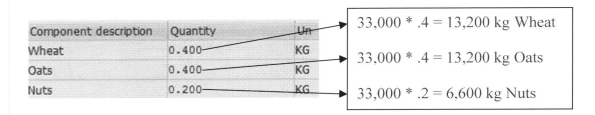

Component description	Quantity	Un
Wheat	0.400	KG
Oats	0.400	KG
Nuts	0.200	KG

33,000 * .4 = 13,200 kg Wheat

33,000 * .4 = 13,200 kg Oats

33,000 * .2 = 6,600 kg Nuts

In addition to planning the purchase of raw materials, MRP also creates a *planned production order*.

To see your *planned production order*, visit the Stock Requirements List:

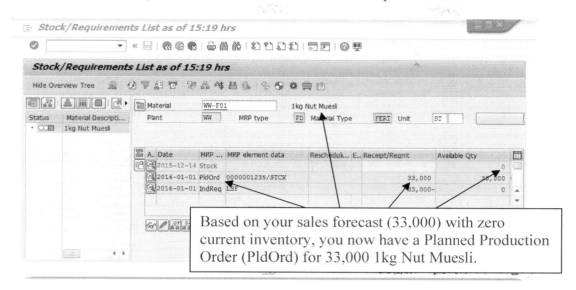

Based on your sales forecast (33,000) with zero current inventory, you now have a Planned Production Order (PldOrd) for 33,000 1kg Nut Muesli.

MRP looks at your forecast, looks at your ingredients list (or BOM), looks at the finished goods (including goods in-process or scheduled for production) and raw materials in stock, and then *plans* for which raw materials to order, how many of each raw material to order, and it creates a corresponding *planned* production order.

Quite Simply, MRP is Complicated

The above example simplifies MRP. Within the Manufacturing Game Simulation, once you are several days or rounds into the simulation, it gets more complicated. Consider a more complicated ERPsim MRP run on Round 1, Day 20 with three products and an adjusted sales forecast of 100,000.

1kg Nut Muesli	
Sales Forecast	100,000
Unsold Inventory	25,000
Scheduled Production	25,000
Raw Material Inventory	0

What is the quantity for the *planned production order*?

The forecast is for 100,000 finished 1kg Nut Muesli. The current inventory is 25,000. There are 25,000 scheduled to be produced. MRP takes the forecast of 100,000, subtracts 25,000 of current inventory, and another 25,000 of in-process finished goods inventory.

The planned production order will be for 50,000 units of 1kg Nut Muesli.

What is the quantity for each *purchase requisition*?

In order to produce 50,000 units of 1kg Nut Muesli, with no raw material inventory, the inventory for all 50,000 units must be purchased.

The five purchase requisitions for 50,000 1kg Nut Muesli will show these quantities:

1Large Box – 50,000 * 1 = 50,000
1Large Bag – 50,000 * 1 = 50,000
.4kg Wheat – 50,000 * .4 = 20,000
.4kg Oats – 50,000 * .4 = 20,000
.2kg Nuts – 50,000 * .2 = 10,000

Wait, You Said MRP is Complicated...

While the above example is only slightly more complicated than the initial example, consider running MRP for 6 products, varying inventory levels of finished goods and raw materials, and a number of finished goods scheduled for production.

Now think about a large company with 1000s of products requiring 1000s of parts per product.

It's in this situation that MRP within an ERP system shines, and increases efficiency. It's the simplicity of the manufacturing game which makes it easier to understand MRP, ERP systems, and how they are beneficial to a company's overall strategy.

Planning!

Remember, that MRP is nothing but *planning*. If all you do is run MRP, no raw materials will be ordered, and nothing will be produced. You just have a plan. Run it again, you have a new plan.

In order to manufacture something, you have to take the *plan* and convert those *plans* into actual orders.

Section 04 - Production

Production: Manufacturing Finished Goods

After running MRP, you have a plan; nothing but a plan.

By running MRP, no raw materials will be ordered and nothing will be produced. Run MRP over and over, and all you have is a new set of plans.

But, when you're ready to execute the plan, how do you execute it?

Within SAP there are many ways to make this happen. This chapter will follow the process as it relates to the ERPsim Manufacturing Game. We'll use the ERPsim game as the example throughout this section, specifically referencing the Manufacturing Game's Job Aid and the actual transactions required to complete production within the simulation.

Converting Purchase Requisitions to Purchase Orders

While there are many ways to convert *Purchase Requisitions* to *Purchase Orders* within SAP, for the purposes of ERPsim's Manufacturing Game, one transaction will make this conversion: ME59N.

From the Job Aid:

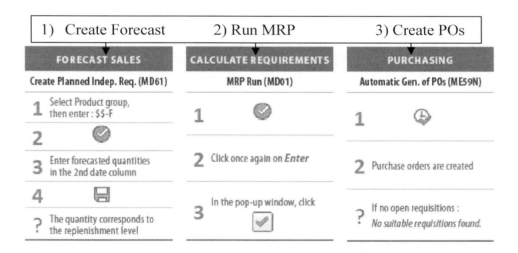

Creating a forecast was covered within Section 2. Running MRP was covered within Section 3. If you're not sure how we've reached this part of the process, re-read those two sections and then continue.

After the forecast has been entered, and after MRP has been run, you have a list of *Purchase Requisitions*. By running the transaction ME59N, all of the open *Purchase Requisitions* are consolidated and converted into *Purchase Orders*.

Like running MRP, this is a simple transaction. And nothing really seems to happen. However, behind the scenes, open *Purchase Requisitions* have been converted into consolidated *Purchase Orders*.

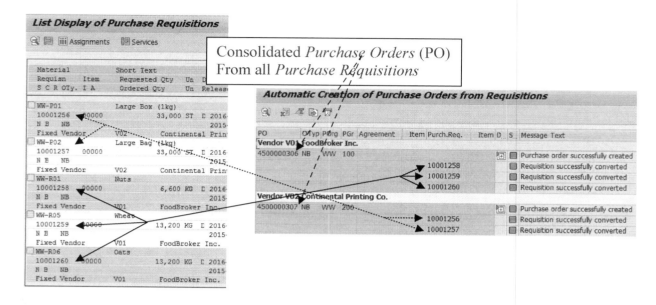

The following is an abbreviated view of the consolidated PO for FoodBroker, Inc.:

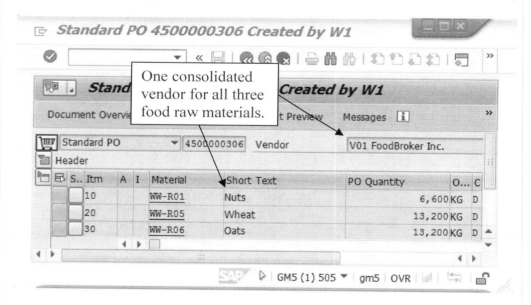

All of this happens automatically, and behind the scenes.

You Have Purchase Orders, Now What?

Within the "real world", these *Purchase Orders* would need to be officially placed as orders with the preferred vendor. This can take place electronically, by phone, by email, etc. The *Purchase Order* is simply a log of the original order, and the sales transaction. Many vendors expect a PO

Number, the document number for this *Purchase Order,* within their internal *Sales Order.* Within the above example, the PO Number is "4500001017". This number is referenced within all related communication between the vendor and organization placing the order.

However, while this is relevant and necessary within the "real world", it is not relevant within the ERPsim Manufacturing Game. Vendor management, submitting the order for raw materials, the receipt of those goods, and all related bookkeeping is automated.

Lead-time. Just Like the "Real World"

Few vendors provide goods instantly. Especially tangible goods like the raw materials within the ERPsim Manufacturing Game. Simulating the real world, POs have been placed with the vendor, and now you must wait for the vendor to ship and deliver those raw materials. This is referred to as vendor *Lead Time*.

Looking at the Manufacturing Game's Job Aid, we see that the lead time is between 3 and 5 simulated days:

General Information

CUSTOMERS			
	DC10	**DC12**	**DC14**
Payment time (days)	20	10-15	5-15

SUPPLIERS	
Lead time (days)	3-5
Payment time (days)	15

FIXED COSTS (paid each 5 days)	
Direct labor	€21 120
Factory overhead	€14 400
S, G & A	€46 400

Default Production Capacity

24,000 units/day

Note that this is the same lead-time you utilized within Section 2 to calculate your initial Sales Forecast.

Because you can't manufacture anything until the raw materials have been delivered, you need a report to tell you when they will be delivered, and a confirmation for the raw material delivery. ERPsim has created a customized SAP report which tracks *Purchase Orders*.

From the Job Aid:

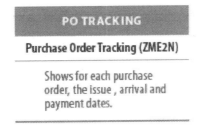

Running transaction ZME2N brings a customized report with your company's *Purchase Orders.*

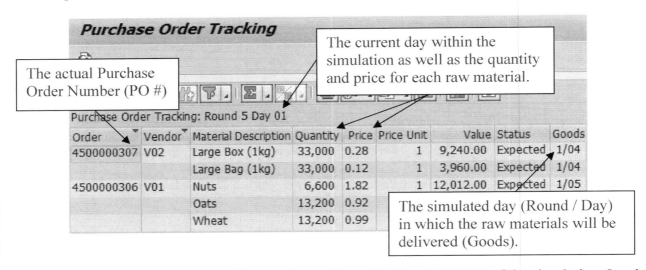

Note that "Goods", the raw materials, are due on Round 1, Day 4 (R1D4) of the simulation. Lead time is between 3 and 5 days. At this particular time, FoodBrokers, Inc. will be delivering the raw materials 4 days after ordering while Continental Printing will be delivering 5 days after.

How do you know when the raw materials have been delivered? Because you cannot start manufacturing until all of the raw materials have been delivered, it's important to know exactly when they are available. While you could watch the inventory report, the Purchase Order Tracking Report will tell you exactly when those raw materials have been delivered.

Note the "Status" column within the report. Right now the goods are listed as "Expected". Once the raw materials have been delivered, and are officially ready for production, the column will display "Delivered" clearly indicating delivery completion.

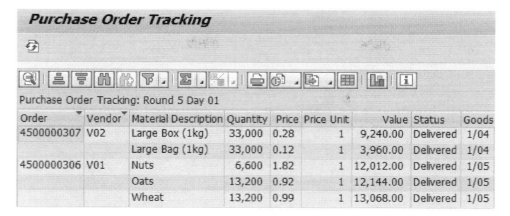

Purchase Order Tracking

Purchase Order Tracking: Round 5 Day 01

Order	Vendor	Material Description	Quantity	Price	Price Unit	Value	Status	Goods
4500000307	V02	Large Box (1kg)	33,000	0.28	1	9,240.00	Delivered	1/04
		Large Bag (1kg)	33,000	0.12	1	3,960.00	Delivered	1/04
4500000306	V01	Nuts	6,600	1.82	1	12,012.00	Delivered	1/05
		Oats	13,200	0.92	1	12,144.00	Delivered	1/05
		Wheat	13,200	0.99	1	13,068.00	Delivered	1/05

Receiving Raw Materials is Easy!

Again, ERPsim has simplified things. Within an actual company using SAP, someone would need to receive the raw materials, confirm their quantities, and compare the delivered materials and quantities within the order. This *Goods Receipt* would directly reference the original *Purchase Order*. Typically, one person would place the order while someone else would receive the order. This helps to cut down on internal fraud—one person orders, one person receives. Hopefully the two aren't in collusion.

Within SAP, the person receiving has to individually check each raw material and confirm the quantity. In addition, they need to note where within the warehouse the raw material is being stored. For a large company, there could be 100s of warehouse storage locations. Within ERPsim, there are only a few locations.

The following is the SAP transaction someone in receiving would use to acknowledge receipt of the raw materials from a *Purchase Order*:

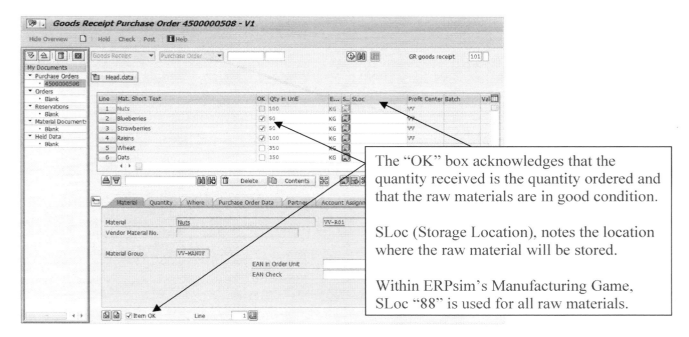

The "OK" box acknowledges that the quantity received is the quantity ordered and that the raw materials are in good condition.

SLoc (Storage Location), notes the location where the raw material will be stored.

Within ERPsim's Manufacturing Game, SLoc "88" is used for all raw materials.

Again, this is all automated while the simulation is running. When "Delivered" appears within the "Status" column of the Purchase Order Tracking Report, the raw materials are now in stock and available for production.

I Have My Raw Materials, Now What?

Remember that MRP plans for production. MRP looks at your sales forecast, then looks at your raw materials and in-process finished goods, and then creates a *plan* to produce enough products to meet your sales forecast.

This plan includes two different parts: *planned purchase orders* and *planned production orders*.

The planned purchase orders are the *Purchase Requisitions* that are converted into *Purchase Orders*. The planned production order is a *Planned Order* which can be converted into a *Production Order* once the raw materials are available.

Within SAP, there are many ways to convert *Planned Orders* into *Production Orders*. You can manually convert them, or you can automatically convert several orders at once. For speed and simplicity, the ERPsim Manufacturing Game prefers mass conversion of *Planned Orders*.

From the Job Aid:

RELEASE PRODUCTION

Coll. Conversion of Pld Orders (CO41)

1 ⊕

? If no planned order: *Planned order could not be selected*

2 Select orders

3 Click on *Convert*. Message confirms the conversion.

? If conversion fails, click on ✂ to see log

Following our example of 1kg Nut Muesli:

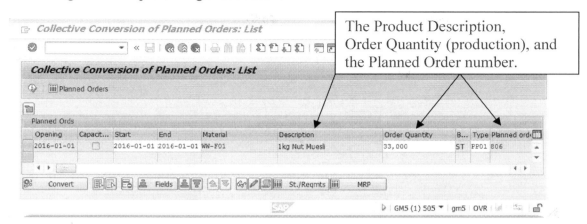

By clicking on the product's line and then clicking the "Convert" button, this *Planned Order* will be converted into a *Production Order*. If everything converts as expected (raw materials are in stock which match the quantity for the Planned order), you'll receive a similar message to this:

☑ Planned order 806 was converted into production order 1000555

Going beyond our example, Transaction Code CO41 is designed to convert multiple *Planned Orders* at once. You can produce in a specific order by choosing and converting one product at a time.

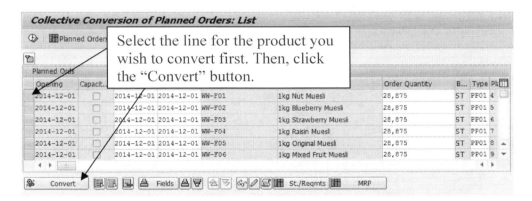

The Production Schedule will be updated based on the order in which you convert these *Planned Orders*. As part of a winning strategy within the Manufacturing Game, it would be a good idea to confirm sales/marketing reports and current stock levels before converting. There's no point in rushing production of a product which is not selling and is currently in stock.

Once you convert the *Planned Orders*, they become *Production Orders*. Your Production Schedule can be viewed using a customized report specifically used within the Manufacturing Game.

From the Job Aid:

This transaction, ZCOOIS, brings up this custom report:

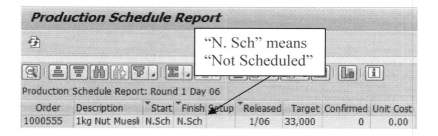

Of course, it's unlikely that you'd only be producing one product with such a small forecast. ZCOOIS will, likely, be filled with multiple production orders:

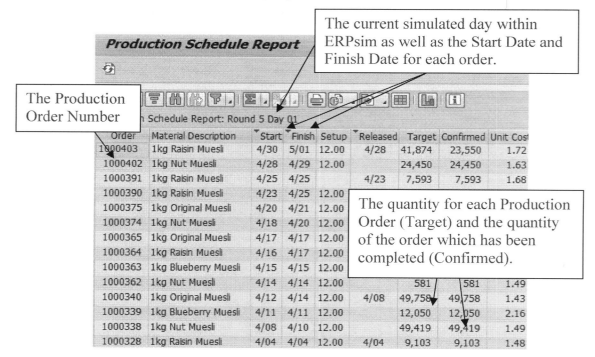

Releasing Production – Strategically

Finished Goods become available for sale as each *Production Order* is confirmed. No sales take place without inventory in stock. There are no "backorders" within the Manufacturing Game.

This is important to note as *Fixed Costs* (the daily expenses) continue even if you do not sell anything. A *Stock Out* of any product means that no sales of that product will take place until that product has been produced.

Reducing *Stock Outs* is part of a winning strategy within the ERPsim Manufacturing Game.

The order in which you convert each product is important; as is considering setup time between products. Does it make sense to release a production order for 2,000? With 12 hours of set-up time, your company will lose half a day's worth of production just to manufacture 2,000 finished goods.

As you learn more about the production process, consider strategies which make for the most efficient production line as is possible.

You've Converted Production, When Do You Run MRP Again?

Remember that your Sales Forecast (from Section 2) is based on what you plan to sell from MRP run to MRP run (Section 3). MRP calculates production orders based on the forecast and existing inventories. When do you run MRP again?

While various Manufacturing Game strategies will lead to different MRP intervals, until you have a feel for your company's strategy, follow "Best Practices" for production:

- As soon as you finish converting all of your production orders, immediately run MRP.

Consistently ordering raw materials to be delivered just ahead of your scheduled production will lead to a more efficient production schedule, or higher productivity. This is important because if you wait until after the last scheduled production order, nothing is being produced. This concept becomes more important as we discuss productivity and net income within a future section. For now, just know that after converting your *Planned Orders* (CO41), you should immediately run MRP (MD01) and convert your *Purchase Requisitions* (ME59N).

As an example, take a look at the following Purchase Order Tracking Report and the corresponding Production Schedule Report.

Note that the raw materials are due to be delivered *before* the production schedule ends. This should always be your goal.

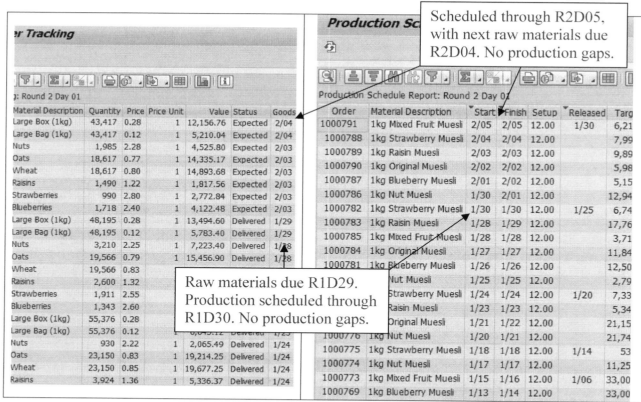

No matter what's happening with sales, you'll always want your production running.

Watch for it – "No Suitable Purchase Requisitions Found"

In a previous example, we ordered enough raw materials to create 33,000 1kg Nut Muesli. Once the raw materials were delivered, had we checked our inventory we would have found that our raw material inventory was updated:

88	WW-P01	Large Box (1kg)	33,000	ST
	WW-P02	Large Bag (1kg)	33,000	ST
	WW-P03	Small Box (500g)	0	ST
	WW-P04	Small Bag (500g)	0	ST
	WW-R01	Nuts	6,600	KG
	WW-R02	Blueberries	0	KG
	WW-R03	Strawberries	0	KG
	WW-R04	Raisins	0	KG
	WW-R05	Wheat	13,200	KG
	WW-R06	Oats	13,200	KG

Within the Manufacturing Game, "best practices" tell us that after converting our planned production orders to *Production Orders* (CO41), we should immediately repeat the production process.

Let's say that immediately after converting our orders (CO41), we run MRP (MD01), and then convert the purchase requisitions to purchase orders (ME59N).

Based on our sales forecast of 33,000, and raw material levels which EXACTLY match the raw material requirements for 33,000 1kg Nut Muesli, and a Production Order for 33,000 1kg Nut Muesli... what do you think will happen?

While MRP will run without an error, the next transaction (ME59N) will give you a message:

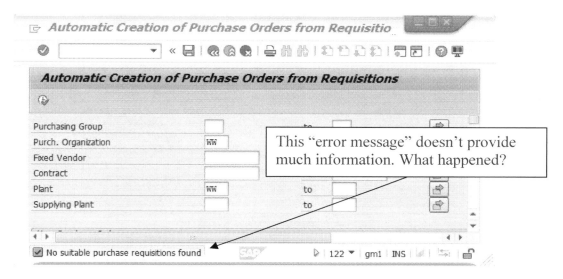

MRP takes everything into consideration—and only plans for what needs planning.

What happened? MRP did nothing. Nothing was planned. The sales forecast has been met—there is no need to order additional raw materials, there is no need to plan for any additional production.

1kg Nut Muesli	
Sales Forecast	33,000
Unsold Inventory	0
Scheduled Production	33,000
Raw Material Inventory	0*

*Why is raw material inventory listed as zero? The raw material shows in inventory, but has been allocated to the production of 33,000 1kg Nut Muesli. The listed raw material has been allocated under "Scheduled Production". Yes, MRP is complicated.

Forecast to Production to Sales

The following details the process and the corresponding SAP transactions required to produce and sell a product.

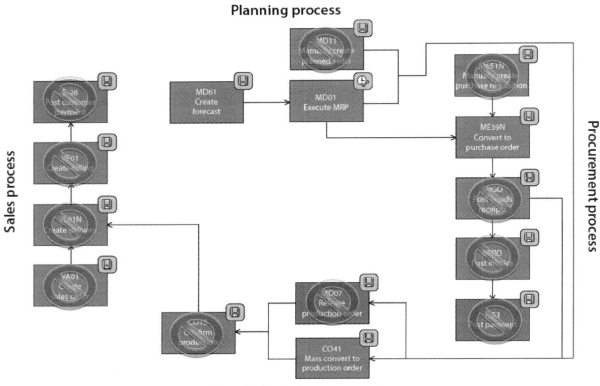

While the ERPsim Extended Manufacturing Game simulation is running, however, only four transactions are required:

1. MD61 – Create Forecast
2. MD01 – Execute MRP
3. ME59N – Convert to Purchase Order
4. CO41 – Mass Convert to Production Order

All other transactions, including sales, shipping, posting of payments, receipt of payments, and all other accounting transactions, are automatically completed by the simulation.

Section 05 - Productivity and Net Income

Is Your Company Profitable?

Within ERPsim's Manufacturing Game, your company's profitability, or net income, is all that matters. Your company is ranked against all other competing teams based on your cumulative net income. It doesn't matter how much you've sold, your market share, nor your production capabilities; it's all about net income.

Without understanding your costs, it's unlikely that you'll be profitable.

How Do I Determine Costs in ERPsim's Manufacturing Game?

There's no easy way to do this. But there is a nice planning report which can help you get a good estimate. From there, it's up to you and your team to calculate more accurate per unit costs.

Transaction ZCK11:

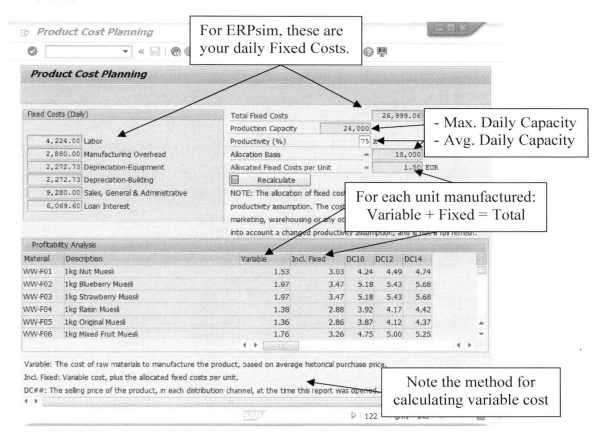

ZCK11 tracks your daily fixed costs and is automatically updated if fixed costs change (investing in your capacity, changes to your loan's balance, etc.).

Your Company's Productivity and Profitability

Section 05
Productivity and Net Income

Following the basic accounting premise that Revenue – Expenses = Profit (Net Income), to achieve positive net income, your selling price (revenue) must consistently exceed all costs (expenses). Increasing your profitability requires one of two things: raising price (revenue) or reducing costs (expenses).

Raising your price is "easy", but will it yield results? If you're the only company selling a certain product, raising your price may work. You may continue to sell your product at a more profitable rate. In a competitive market, if you try to raise your price you may need to invest in marketing—which also increases expenses. How much marketing will allow you to raise your price, without reducing too much of your profits? All expenses must be closely monitored.

Reducing expenses below your price also increases your profitability.

Within the ERPsim Manufacturing Game, your variable costs include the costs of raw materials, marketing, warehousing capacity, and any other expenses you might incur. Reduction of these expenses requires watching raw material prices, limiting warehouse capacity expenses, and making good business decisions throughout the game. Unfortunately, the cost of doing business often requires these variable costs—and there's not much you can do if your most profitable product includes a raw material which has increased in price throughout the simulation.

While there are ways to reduce your variable costs, which your company should explore, the most consistent way to reduce costs is to reduce your fixed costs.

Fixed costs within ERPsim include the following categories:

Amount	Category
4,224.00	Labor
2,880.00	Manufacturing Overhead
2,272.73	Depreciation-Equipment
2,272.73	Depreciation-Building
9,280.00	Sales, General & Administrative
6,069.60	Loan Interest

With no changes to your loan amount or capacity, these fixed costs stay the same throughout the simulation. While they are listed above as "daily", ERPsim automatically pays/expenses them every five days.

How do you Reduce a Fixed Cost?

While it's possible to pay down your loan (which reduces your loan interest expense), fixed costs are… fixed. No matter what you do, your fixed costs will stay the same throughout the simulation.

There is, however, a way to *reduce* your per unit cost. It's quite simple to identify, but not so simple to execute: your fixed cost allocation basis. Increase the number of units your company can manufacture and your per unit cost is reduced. The fixed costs are spread out across additional units, reducing fixed cost per unit.

Without investments, your production capacity starts at 24,000 units per day. This is reduced by mandatory setup time between products. Without investments, your starting setup time is 12 hours between products.

By default, the cost planning tool (ZCK11) starts at 75% productivity. This starting percentage presumes that your daily production will run 75% of the time, or 18 out-of-the 24 hours available each day for production. Your company's actual productivity will vary depending on your strategy. However, knowing your productivity % is crucial to determining the most profitable price for your product.

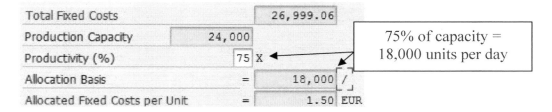

Total Fixed Costs		26,999.06	
Production Capacity	24,000		
Productivity (%)	75 X		
Allocation Basis	=	18,000	/
Allocated Fixed Costs per Unit	=	1.50	EUR

75% of capacity = 18,000 units per day

Spreading the daily fixed costs across 75% of the starting capacity allocates costs of 1.50€ per unit. The cost planning tool allows you to adjust this percentage to test various productivity scenarios. What happens if you produce at 50% of capacity?

Total Fixed Costs		26,999.06	
Production Capacity	24,000		
Productivity (%)	50 X		
Allocation Basis	=	12,000	/
Allocated Fixed Costs per Unit	=	2.25	EUR

Per unit costs increase from 1.50€ to 2.25€! It is unlikely that you'll be competitive with per unit costs that are this high. But, what if you reach maximum productivity?

Total Fixed Costs		26,999.06	
Production Capacity	24,000		
Productivity (%)	99 X		
Allocation Basis	=	23,760	/
Allocated Fixed Costs per Unit	=	1.14	EUR

While 100% is the maximum, ZCK11 only allows 2 digits—so we use 99%. But, what a difference this makes! Down from 1.50€ to 1.14€!

How much profit will you earn per unit sold? ZCK11 also shows each of your six potential finished products, uses a historical average to calculate the variable cost (using the current BOM for each product), and then gives a unit Total Cost based on your Allocated Fixed Cost per Unit estimation.

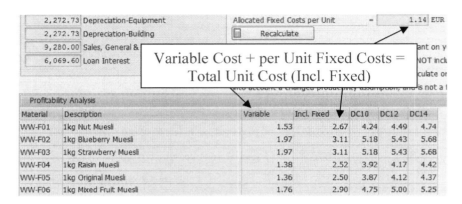

While changing prices is within transaction VK32, ZCK11 offers a nice cost/price comparison using your current product prices. Your prices follow the three distribution channels and all three prices are listed within ZCK11. (Note: 1kg boxes are only sold in DC10 and DC12 while 500g boxes are only sold within DC12 and DC14.)

Within ZCK11, you can compare your current prices with your estimated productivity % and allocated unit costs. Are you staying profitable?

At 50%	At 75%	At 99%	Current Prices	
Incl. Fixed	Incl. Fixed	Incl. Fixed	DC10	DC12
3.78	3.03	2.67	4.24	4.49
4.22	3.47	3.11	5.18	5.43
4.22	3.47	3.11	5.18	5.43
3.63	2.88	2.52	3.92	4.17
3.61	2.86	2.50	3.87	4.12
4.01	3.26	2.90	4.75	5.00

Is 50% productivity profitable at the current prices? Yes, but those are some tight margins. Any miscalculation in additional expenses, a stock-out, or other unplanned circumstances could lead to negative net income.

However, 99% productivity shows that all six products are selling at a healthy profit-margin. Provided that sales can keep up with these prices within a competitive market, 99% productivity is certainly the most profitable of the above examples.

What's my Productivity?

Without using external Business Intelligence tools, you can only estimate your productivity during game play. You can estimate it by looking at your Production Schedule (ZCOOIS) and estimating the down-time you're experiencing on your production line. Any days without productivity are 0/24 within your running productivity average. Switching between products also requires setup time, which means no productivity. This is listed as "Setup" within the Production Schedule Report:

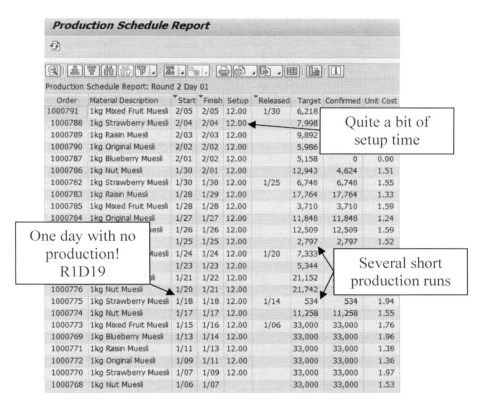

Your exact productivity % can only be estimated here, but you can look through this production schedule and see some BIG productivity issues. The two biggest issues with this company's productivity include a day with no production (R1D19) and the short production runs—with the full 12 hour setup time between them and the next product.

Consider an estimate of your daily productivity goal. Starting capacity is 24,000 per day, with 12 hours of setup time between products. To achieve a goal of 50% productivity, your production runs would need to be 12,000 per day. Looking at the above schedule, a production run of 534 with setup time of 12 hours immediately after will yield productivity far less than 50%. How many production runs are less than 12,000, below 50%? Of the 24 listed production orders, 12 are less than 12,000. Only 12 of the production orders exceed the daily capacity of 24,000.

Without attempting to calculate the productivity % for this company, it is safe to say that it is below 50% productivity. It is unlikely that this company is achieving positive net income.

What is this company's actual productivity %? ERPsim provides end of round results between rounds. The ERPsim viewer provides this information for all participating teams. Ask your instructor for access to your simulation's viewer.

> Note: The viewer only provides cumulative and per round information. Historical information is not kept. Nor is this information available after the simulation has completed. If you are interested in this information, you'll want to copy and paste the information or take a screen shot and save it. Otherwise, you will not have this information again.

Looking at the end of round results for this particular team, which has been our example team throughout much of this text, it is not doing well:

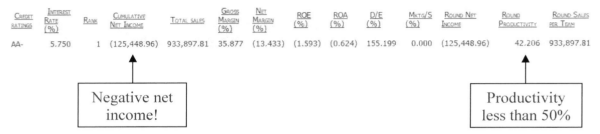

Credit Ratings	Interest Rate (%)	Rank	Cumulative Net Income	Total Sales	Gross Margin (%)	Net Margin (%)	ROE (%)	ROA (%)	D/E (%)	Mktg/S (%)	Round Net Income	Round Productivity	Round Sales per Team
AA-	5.750	1	(125,448.96)	933,897.81	35.877	(13.433)	(1.593)	(0.624)	155.199	0.000	(125,448.96)	42.206	933,897.81

Negative net income!

Productivity less than 50%

Let's plug this team's actual productivity % into ZCK11 and see what happens:

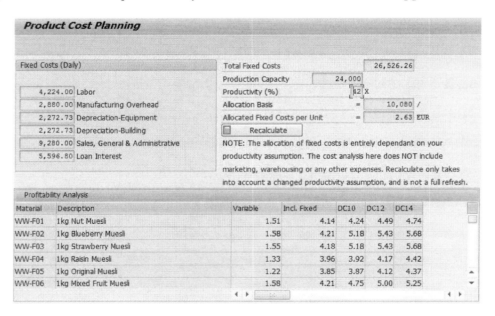

Is there a surprise that this team has negative net income? Given their productivity within Round 1, one of their products is selling under cost, two are close, and the other three are selling at a tight margin. It is no surprise that this team has earned negative net income.

Productivity makes a huge difference to your company's bottom line. Always. Be. Producing.

Section 05
Productivity and Net Income

Frequently Asked Questions

My Productivity is Low. What Can I Do?

If you have too many days without production, you'll need to find a way to produce more often. This might be running the production process more often, or it may be adjusting your sales forecast. If your issue is short production runs with long setup time between products, you have three options: decrease your setup time, skip converting small production runs, or adjust your forecast.

Aside from decreasing setup time, the other two options involve adjusting your sales forecast. Your goal should always be to sell what you're producing each day. Given your capacity and setup time limitations, you can't produce all six products each day, which means that you need to adjust your sales forecast based on which products are actually selling.

There are multiple ways to determine which products are selling and which are not. It is up to you and your team to analyze the many reports to decide this.

How do I Achieve 100% Productivity?

What's the one way to produce with no set up time reductions?

I Have a Lot of Cash—Why do I Have Negative Net Income?

Financial Statement Item/Account	Tot.rpt.pr	tot.cmp.pr
▾ 🗁 Balance Sheet	0.00	0.00
▾ 🗁 Assets	20,095,790.30	20,095,790.30
▾ 🗁 Current assets	3,232,154.04	3,232,154.04
▾ 🗊 113300 Bank Cash Account	2,223,924.56	2,223,924.56
▸ 🎝 YY Company Y	2,223,924.56	2,223,924.56
▸ 🗊 140000 Customers - Domestic Recei	748,999.78	748,999.78
▸ 🗊 300000 Raw materials	87,666.68	
▸ 🗊 792000 Finished goods	171,563.02	
▸ 🗀 Long-term assets	16,863,636.26	
▸ 🗀 Liabilities and Owners' Equity	20,095,790.30-	
▾ 🗁 Income Statement	125,448.96	
▸ 🗀 Revenues	933,897.81-	933,897.81-
▸ 🗀 Cost of Goods Sold	598,842.87	598,842.87
▸ 🗀 Sales, General, and Administrative Expense	460,503.90	460,503.90
▾ 🗁 Net Income(Loss)	125,448.96-	125,448.96-
⸱ Calculated Result	125,448.96-	125,448.96-

> 2.2 million in cash
>
> Neg. Net Income

ERPsim uses accrual basis accounting. Your company uses cash to conduct business and (revenues) minus (expenses) to calculate net income. Dig out your old accounting notes/textbooks, talk to your accounting professor, or look up "accrual basis accounting" online.

I Invested in Setup Time Reduction – Now I have Negative Net Income!

Setup time reduction is an expense. You're, essentially, paying a consultant to help you with lean manufacturing techniques. Payments to consultants are expensed at the time the services are rendered. Within ERPsim, this expense takes place as soon as you save the FB50 transaction.

I Invested in Capacity – Why do I have Positive Net Income?

Investment in capacity is a capital expense. Capital expenses are depreciated over time. Depreciation expenses are automatically expensed every 5 days.

I Invested in Capacity – Why do I Still Have Warehouse Expenses?

Investment in capacity is for your production capacity only. Warehouse expenses come from exceeding your *warehouse* capacity. Additional capacity is automatically expensed daily when additional warehouse space is required.

From the job aid:

Additional storage costs
(billed automatically)

STORAGE COSTS		
Product type	**Current space**	**Cost for additional space**
Finished product	250,000 boxes	€250/day for each add. 25,000 boxes
Raw materials	250,000 kg	€500/day for each add. 25,000 kg
Packaging (bags and boxes)	1,000,000 units	€100/day for each add. 25,000 units

Section 06 - Logistics

The following section pertains to the ERPsim Advanced Manufacturing Game. Unless your instructor has chosen to include this ERPsim game into your course, there is no need to read this section.

One Major Difference

The ERPsim Advanced Manufacturing Game is nearly the same as the Extended Manufacturing Game. As a company, you and your team are responsible for procuring raw materials, producing finished goods, utilizing reports to determine sales trends, and updating pricing and marketing accordingly. What's different? Logistics.

Within the Advanced Manufacturing Game, not only do you have to produce and sell the finished goods, you also have to figure out how those products will get to your customers.

Regions and Storage Locations

As you know from within the Extended Manufacturing Game, the German market is divided into three regions: North, South, and West. There are also three Distribution Channels (DCs): 10, 12, and 14.

Within the Advanced Manufacturing Game, your finished goods are produced and stored within a main warehouse, but each region has its own storage location—customers are not permitted to buy directly from the main warehouse, nor from a storage location outside of their geographic area.

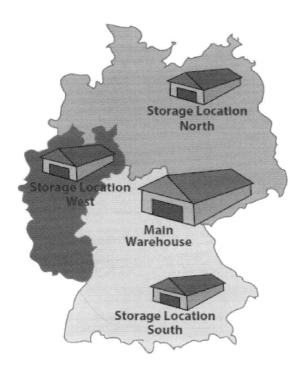

New Storage Locations

Each regional customer must purchase finished goods from a regional storage location. Each regional storage location is noted within SAP Transaction: ZMB52

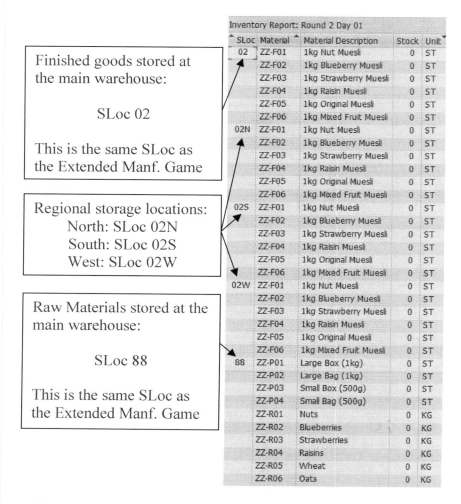

Finished goods stored at the main warehouse:

SLoc 02

This is the same SLoc as the Extended Manf. Game

Regional storage locations:
North: SLoc 02N
South: SLoc 02S
West: SLoc 02W

Raw Materials stored at the main warehouse:

SLoc 88

This is the same SLoc as the Extended Manf. Game

SLoc	Material	Material Description	Stock	Unit
02	ZZ-F01	1kg Nut Muesli	0	ST
	ZZ-F02	1kg Blueberry Muesli	0	ST
	ZZ-F03	1kg Strawberry Muesli	0	ST
	ZZ-F04	1kg Raisin Muesli	0	ST
	ZZ-F05	1kg Original Muesli	0	ST
	ZZ-F06	1kg Mixed Fruit Muesli	0	ST
02N	ZZ-F01	1kg Nut Muesli	0	ST
	ZZ-F02	1kg Blueberry Muesli	0	ST
	ZZ-F03	1kg Strawberry Muesli	0	ST
	ZZ-F04	1kg Raisin Muesli	0	ST
	ZZ-F05	1kg Original Muesli	0	ST
	ZZ-F06	1kg Mixed Fruit Muesli	0	ST
02S	ZZ-F01	1kg Nut Muesli	0	ST
	ZZ-F02	1kg Blueberry Muesli	0	ST
	ZZ-F03	1kg Strawberry Muesli	0	ST
	ZZ-F04	1kg Raisin Muesli	0	ST
	ZZ-F05	1kg Original Muesli	0	ST
	ZZ-F06	1kg Mixed Fruit Muesli	0	ST
02W	ZZ-F01	1kg Nut Muesli	0	ST
	ZZ-F02	1kg Blueberry Muesli	0	ST
	ZZ-F03	1kg Strawberry Muesli	0	ST
	ZZ-F04	1kg Raisin Muesli	0	ST
	ZZ-F05	1kg Original Muesli	0	ST
	ZZ-F06	1kg Mixed Fruit Muesli	0	ST
88	ZZ-P01	Large Box (1kg)	0	ST
	ZZ-P02	Large Bag (1kg)	0	ST
	ZZ-P03	Small Box (500g)	0	ST
	ZZ-P04	Small Bag (500g)	0	ST
	ZZ-R01	Nuts	0	KG
	ZZ-R02	Blueberries	0	KG
	ZZ-R03	Strawberries	0	KG
	ZZ-R04	Raisins	0	KG
	ZZ-R05	Wheat	0	KG
	ZZ-R06	Oats	0	KG

Inventory Report: Round 2 Day 01

Remember: regional customers can ONLY purchase from your regional storage locations

Warehouse capacity restrictions apply, across all SLoc/Storage Locations, regardless of the warehouse's regional location:

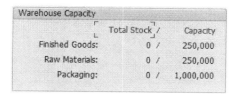

Warehouse Capacity	Total Stock /	Capacity
Finished Goods:	0 /	250,000
Raw Materials:	0 /	250,000
Packaging:	0 /	1,000,000

Just like within the Extended Manufacturing Game, your company will automatically be charged if you exceed your warehouse capacity. The charges for additional warehouse space are listed on the Advanced Manufacturing Game's Job Aid.

Moving Inventory from the Main Warehouse to the Regional Storage Locations

Customers can only purchase from regional storage locations, regardless of what is in stock at the main warehouse or other regional storage locations. So, how do you get your finished goods to the regional storage locations?

Transaction Code: ZMB1B:

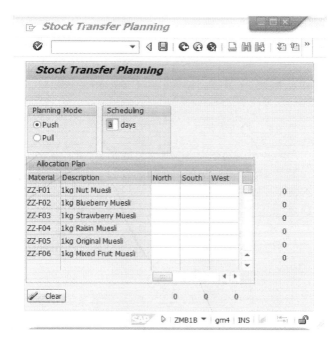

This transaction may not look like much, but there are multiple MAJOR decision points to be made. Let's look at each section of the transaction one-by-one.

Push or Pull?

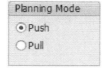

The Planning Mode covers two strategies for sending finished goods to the regional storage locations. Which strategy is best? It depends. Let's define the two strategies:

> **Push** – At a regular interval, your main warehouse sends a specified amount of finished goods to each of the regional storage locations. Finished goods are "pushed" to each regional storage location, regardless of the regional location's current stock level.
>
> As an example, every 3 days the main warehouse may send 2500 finished goods to the regional storage location, regardless of the storage location's current inventory.

Pull – At a regular interval, your main warehouse assesses the current inventory of each regional storage location and only stocks enough inventory to meet the listed stock level.

As an example, every 3 days the main warehouse will assess the regional storage location's current inventory and send just enough finished goods to meet the specified inventory level. If the level is set for 2000, and the regional warehouse has 500, 1500 of the finished good will be sent to the regional warehouse.

How Often?

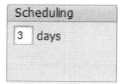

How often do you "Push" or "Pull" your finished goods to the regional storage locations?

There is no right or wrong answer. However, each time you send finished products to each location, it costs 100€ per location. Too often and the expenses eat into your net income. Less often and you risk a stock out (remember, regional customers can only purchase from your regional storage location).

In order to determine how often you send products to your warehouse, you'll want to watch the sales reports. What's selling? How much is selling? Where is it selling? Factor in your production capacity and sales forecast—can you deliver on time?

This may seem like an easy decision, but it's not. Too often and you risk increased expenses which reduce your net income. Not often enough and you risk a stock out in a region.

Plan wisely. Make changes as necessary.

How Many of each Finished Product to each Region?

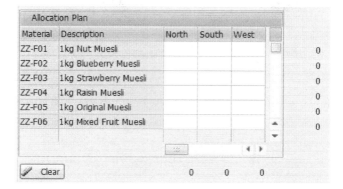

You have six possible finished goods. You have three regions. How much do you push or pull to each region? This number needs to work together with your sales forecast, and how much you plan to sell in each region. Remember that every time the simulation is run, a certain geographic area has a preference for a certain product. It's up to you to determine what is selling and in which region. You may sell 1000s per day in one region, and 100s per day of the same product in another region. You'll need to watch the sales reports to determine what is selling, and how much is desired in each region.

Think About Your Capacity

With the standard capacity to produce 24,000 finished goods per day and set up time between products of 12 hours, you are limited to how much your company can produce every day.

With multiple finished goods and the required set up time, your company should expect to manufacture the minimum each day:

24,000 [daily capacity] * .5 [12 hours setup time] = 12,000 [finished goods per day]

What if the following is your "Push" strategy?

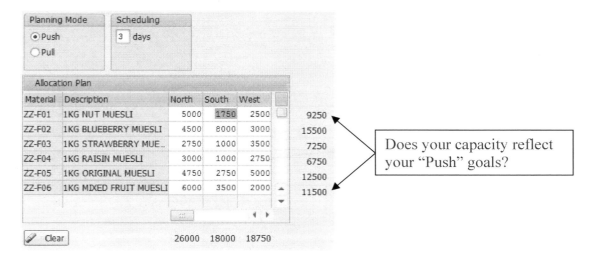

Does your capacity reflect your "Push" goals?

Using the above example, your company expects to "Push" (9,250 + 15,500 + 7,250 + 6,750 + 12,500 + 11,500) = 62,750 finished goods every three days. Yet, your capacity and setup time states that your average three-day manufacturing capacity is 12,000 * 3 = 36,000.

Based on your company's current capacity and setup time, you should only expect to push about 36,000 every 3 days. You can't possibly meet the above "Push" strategy.

Don't Forget Your Sales Forecast!

Your sales forecast should also reflect how much you plan to "Push" or "Pull" within your scheduled stock transfer planning. If you forecast under the amount you plan to "Push" or "Pull", you won't have enough finished goods to send to the regional warehouses. If you forecast over the amount, you're leaving finished goods in your main warehouse. No customer can purchase from your main warehouse, and too many finished goods equals added warehouse expenses.

Watch your sales forecast! Adjust as necessary.

FAQ

When I send inventory to a storage location, am I charged 100€ per product, per location?

You are charged 100€ each time you ship from the main warehouse to the regional storage location. It is 100€ regardless of how much or how little you send.

What is the capacity when shipping to a regional storage location?

There is no capacity for shipping between the main warehouse and the regional storage locations. You are able to send as much as or as little as you'd like each time you send product to a storage location.

How do I move inventory from one regional storage location to another?

You cannot move inventory from one regional storage location to another. Keep this in mind when planning your strategy. If you send too much and it doesn't sell... it's stuck there.

Are shipments to regional storage locations consolidated?

Yes, every time you ship the allocated products to a regional storage location, all scheduled products will ship at once. You will be charged 100€ per shipment regardless of how much or how little you send.

How do I increase the warehouse capacity?

Within the ERPsim Manufacturing Game, your warehouse capacity is automatically increased once you exceed your warehouse capacity. Check the job aid for these associated costs

Selected Step-by-Step Instructions

Job Aid

The Job Aid for ERPsim games is a great / quick way to find the relevant transactions required for ERPsim game-play. However, if you are new to SAP, the abbreviated instructions may not be intuitive. The following are Step-by-Step instructions for some of the more complicated or less-used transactions.

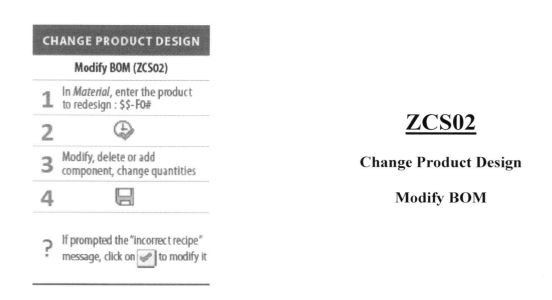

ZCS02

Change Product Design

Modify BOM

Within this example, we'll be changing the 1kg Nut Muesli to 500g Strawberry Muesli.

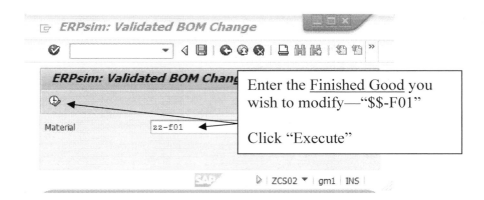

As a "best practice", start by deleting any unwanted components.

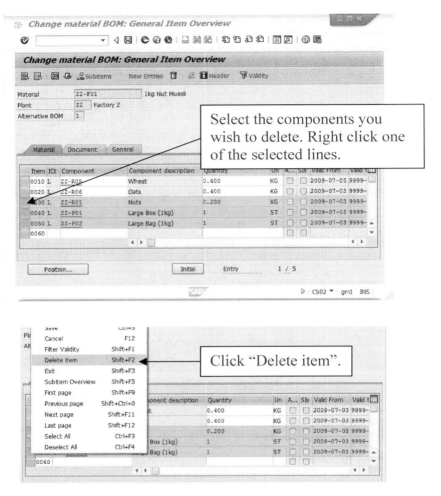

If you receive the question, "Certain selected components are allocated to a task list."

Click enter.

Click "Yes" to delete the selected items.

Next, add the components that are part of your new recipe.

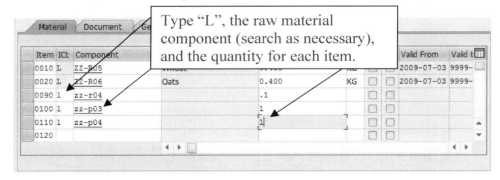

Press "Enter" to fill in the "Component description", and to confirm that you've typed the correct information. If you have any errors, correct them, delete them, or back out and start over.

Next, correct the quantities to reflect the new recipe. Remember to follow MMA guidelines for recipe content. Be sure that your box/bag size match your recipe (1kg vs 500g).

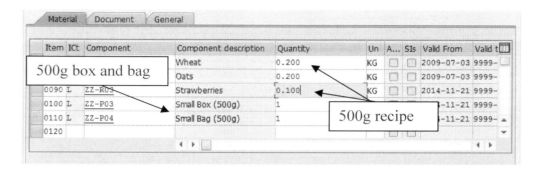

Before you SAVE, click enter to validate your entries!

Fix all errors before saving or closing this transaction!

Click "Save". The SAP transaction will confirm that your recipe meets MMA guidelines. If guidelines are met, the label for your product will automatically update.

☑ Material ZZ-F01 has a valid 500g Strawberry Muesli recipe.

FB50

Loan Repayment

Enter G/L Account

Within the following example, we'll pay down our loan by 100,000€.

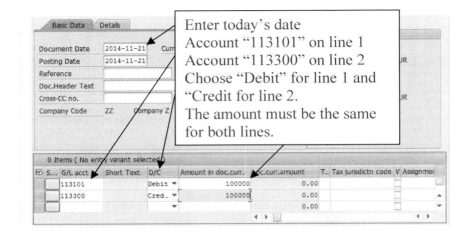

Enter today's date
Account "113101" on line 1
Account "113300" on line 2
Choose "Debit" for line 1 and "Credit for line 2.
The amount must be the same for both lines.

Click "Enter" to confirm details.

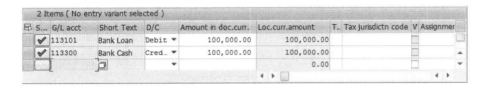

If no errors, click "Save".

Confirm this entry in F.01.

Note: Reverse the debits/credits to *increase* your loan amount with no penalties.

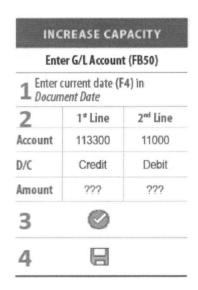

FB50

Increase Capacity

Enter G/L Account

Within the following example, we'll increase our capacity by 100,000€.

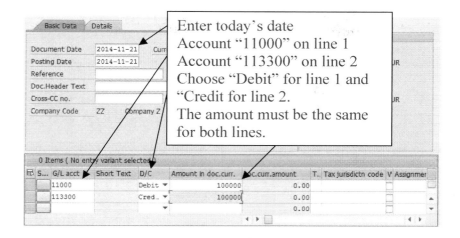

Enter today's date
Account "11000" on line 1
Account "113300" on line 2
Choose "Debit" for line 1 and
"Credit for line 2.
The amount must be the same
for both lines.

Click "Enter" to confirm details.

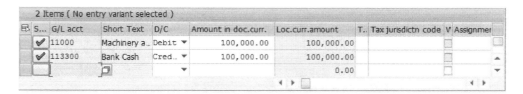

If no errors, click "Save".

Confirm this entry in F.01.

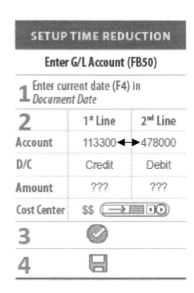

FB50

Setup Time Reduction

Enter G/L Account

Within the following example, we'll reduce our setup time by 100,000€.

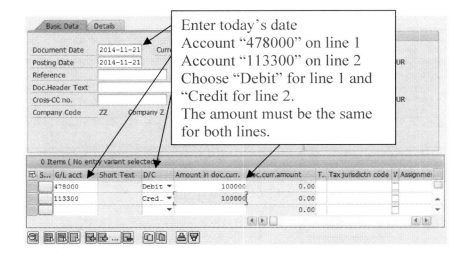

> Enter today's date
> Account "478000" on line 1
> Account "113300" on line 2
> Choose "Debit" for line 1 and
> "Credit for line 2.
> The amount must be the same
> for both lines.

Scroll to the right until you find the field header "Cost Center".

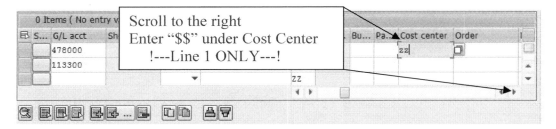

> Scroll to the right
> Enter "$$" under Cost Center
> !---Line 1 ONLY---!

Click "Enter" to confirm details.

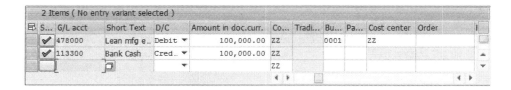

If no errors, click "Save".

Confirm this entry in F.01.

Note: This is an EXPENSE which will reduce your net income.

Relevant Information Form
For Labs 01 through 03

SAP Lab 01

Line	Description	Your Information
1.1	PO Amount – Foodbroker, Inc.	1,128.00 EUR
1.2	PO Number – Foodbroker, Inc.	4500000054
1.3	PO Amount – Continental Printing	400.00 EUR
1.4	PO Number – Continental Printing	4500000055
1.5	Planned Order Number	28
1.6	Production Order Number	1000027

SAP Lab 02

Line	Description	Your Information
2.1	Order's Total Net Value	4,240.00 EUR
2.2	Standard Order #	31
2.3	Outbound Delivery #	80000030

SAP Lab 03

Line	Description	Your Information
3.1	Accounting Invoice Number	0090000028
3.2	2.1 – (1.1+1.3) Sales Order – Total Raw Materials	2,712.00 EUR Net from **Sales – Production**

Made in the USA
Charleston, SC
18 January 2016